The Managerial Odyssey

by Robert L. Focazio

With Andrew Ladd

Illustrations by Austin Mulqueen

Odyssey Publishing

Atlanta, Georgia

Odyssey Books
A Division of Odyssey Publishing
Atlanta, GA

First Printing
Printed in the United States of America
10 9 8 7 6 5 4 3 2 1

Library of Congress Cataloging in Publication Data

Focazio, Robert L
    The Managerial Odyssey
1. Selling 2. Interpersonal Communication. 3. Sales Management I. Focazio, Robert
    L., 1946- II. Ladd, Andrew P., 1964- III. Title

    ISBN 0-9656329-03

Additional copies of *The Managerial Odyssey* may be purchased at;

http://www.amazon.com

The
Managerial
Odyssey

To My Father,
patris est filius

Dad, this is the "more besides" we always
talked about. I know you are someplace close.
You are still the best salesperson I've ever known.
This is my way of saying thanks.
Love, Bob.

Contents

PREFACE ix

INTRODUCTION 1

SECTION ONE:

THREE RULES FOR THE ROAD

Chapter One: All Work and No Play (Makes Life a Dull Bore) 10
When is Motivation an Effective Motivator?—The Top Five
De-motivators—Big Time De-motivators—The Glass is
Always Half Full

Chapter Two: Remember How Good You Are 23
Let Memory Bring the Light of Other Days—What Do You
Mean Failure? Did You See My Last Paycheck?—Remind
Others To Remember How Good They Are

Chapter Three: Take a Risk! 33
Department Stores, Olympic Golds & First Dates—Fear of
Failure or Fear of Failures?—Cincinnati, Here We Come!

SECTION TWO:
THE ART OF BUSINESS

Chapter Four: The Wind-up **51**
Getting Directions—Opening Remarks Open Doors

Chapter Five: The Pitch **65**
Fanning the Fire of Desire—Playing WIIFM Ball—Loading
the Bag—Finding the Zone—Playing the Zone—The Goal
is Victory, Not Persistence

Chapter Six: The Follow-Through **82**
Ignoti Nulla Cupido—The W.W.P.F. Program—I Object!—
Easy as ABC—Closing Remarks

SECTION THREE:
MENTOR MANAGEMENT

Chapter Seven: Debunking Mr. Dithers **99**
Cessante Causa—The Dithers Complex—Making
Mentors—One Caveat Before Moving On

Chapter Eight: Developing Dagwood **116**
Teaching an Old Dagwood New Tricks—Evaluating
Dagwood's Value

Chapter Nine: Empowering Environments **135**
Empowerment Shmowerment—Rule #1: Help them Have
Fun—Rule #2: Treat them with Respect—Rule #3: Give
them Room to Take Risks—Hello, Syracuse

AFTERWORD **150**

APPENDIX **153**

Preface

Most management books today focus entirely too much on process. Don't get me wrong—business process reengineering, total quality management, just-in-time, etc., all have been useful in making the modern corporation more efficient. The problem, however, is that a corporation is only partially made up of processes and structures. The greater part belongs to its *people*. That's why understanding people is a manager's first priority; understanding processes finishes a distant second.

The Managerial Odyssey borrows from a work of literature that understands human kind perhaps better than any other, Homer's Odyssey. I've always felt that the wisdom of the Odyssey lies in its hero's voyage of discovery, and I've tried to recreate that journey here. The way to understanding people must follow a certain path. We have to know ourselves; we have to learn to see from others' points of view; and finally, we need to apply what we've learned to improve our immediate surroundings. Using these ancient principles, this book helps guide today's professionals safely through the many perils of the modern business world.

The Managerial Odyssey issues from hundreds of keynote speeches that I have given to business professionals from around the world. It's also based upon my own 25-plus years experience in sales management, which includes my services as Vice President for AT&T's General Business Systems, now Lucent Technologies, and as Senior Vice President for TIC Enterprises. The book is written for managers interested in winning methods of leadership; individuals committed to outstanding self-management; those seeking a proven, practical sales/management training text; and business leaders interested in learning how to implement a mentor management system that focuses primarily on improving *people.*

This book would not have been possible without a number of creative and talented individuals. My wife Janet provided more than her share of moral support and was an invaluable reader of the book, guiding it from infancy to adolescence and finally to maturity. There have also been a number of others who encouraged me to write this book. They include Erik Jorgensen, my coach at Lucent Technologies; Jim Greiff, perhaps the greatest entrepreneur I know; and my daughter Jennifer, who has always made me proud.

I'd also like to express my gratitude to Odyssey Publishing for their tireless efforts in revising and designing the book and to Austin Mulqueen for his wonderful illustrations. Finally, I'd like to thank Andrew Ladd, a tremendously gifted writer who somehow managed to capture my thoughts on paper.

Introduction

$\mathbf{W}$elcome to the beginning of your odyssey. I mean that in every sense of the word, for what better word than *odyssey* to describe the triumphs and hardships, the trials and errors, the costs and rewards of running a successful business?

Of course you know Homer's famous Odyssey, that ancient and marvelous story of one man's trials endured during his long journey home. For more than 2,000 years this epic of discovery has served as a guidebook for understanding life's travels. Like Homer's Odyssey, *The Managerial Odyssey* is intended to steer you along the right path towards "home," using useful, sound, fun approaches to managing your business . . . and even, perhaps, your life.

Included, necessarily, is quite a lot about my own odyssey, a humble 25-plus-year journey as salesman, division manager, motivational speaker and vice president for AT&T, the world's largest telecommunications company. Drawing upon simple but powerful principles that have brought me and others success, I believe my own experiences will help you define for yourself specific goals and rewards that will bring the level of success you desire.

My intent, then, as author of *The Managerial Odyssey* is to facilitate *your* odyssey. As one of the many people you'll meet during

1

your business travels, I want to help you make important discoveries about yourself, your business, and your people. I hope, therefore, that our encounters in this book will bring you at least a few steps closer to home.

Before we strike out on the path this book follows, I'd like to take a moment to tell you about an exciting discovery I came across a few years ago. That discovery, as you'll see, will give us a head start on the true road to success.

SEEKING THAT MAGIC FORMULA FOR SUCCESS

I'd like to share with you one of the most valuable turns my odyssey has taken to date. The tip I'm about to offer eventually helped me and my company encounter what I like to refer to as *"the magic formula for success."* The information gained from that experience has proven to be one of the single greatest bits of business knowledge we ever acquired, because *it is a sure fire way to gain an edge on the competition.*

It all began a few years ago, back in 1983, while I was working for AT&T as a division manager, responsible for supporting numerous field salespeople. At that time, I was trying to think of ways we could outperform our competitors. An advantage in working for a company like AT&T is that one can draw upon its vast resources for state-of-the-art information.

Realizing that advantage, I called upon our industrial psychologists who work in the Market Research division and posed a challenge: "Listen," I said, "I've got a wacky idea. I'd like to find a way to figure out the personality traits of my customers prior to meeting with them."

If a salesperson could somehow ascertain the personality traits of her customers *before* she presented herself and her services, I reasoned, then she could design her sales presentation to suit the customer's specific personality. If, for example, the customer was aggressive, then the salesperson would be aggressive right back. If he was passive, then she could match his passivity.

The idea had many intriguing possibilities, our Market Research team agreed, so they said, "Okay, Bob, give us six months and we'll get back to you on it." (We study everything for six months. That's just a rule.)

Months later Dr. Dick Richie, our head industrial psychologist, reported back on the study. By now I'd forgotten all about commissioning it.

"Bob, we have the answer!" he said.

"To what?" I asked.

"Do you remember that study you commissioned from us?" he asked.

"Oh, that old idea. I thought you'd moved on to something else by now."

"No, no." he said. "We've got the study results right here. We've developed a test that can identify an individual's personality simply by assessing his or her preferred geometric symbol."

"English, doc, English."

"Okay. In a nutshell, our studies show that you can determine the personality traits of your customers if you observe the geometric symbol with which they surround themselves. Before you ever talk to your customers, you can determine a lot about their personality simply by identifying their predominant geometric symbol."

Skeptical? So was I. "Predominant geometric symbol?!" What a bunch of psychobabble! But, get this: according to the study, the personality test had an accuracy rate of **85%**. I didn't need a Ph.D. in statistics to recognize that, given the unpredictability of human subjects, an 85% success rate is a *substantially* high number for predicting human behavior.

If we could accomplish even half of what the study promised, we'd have a tremendous advantage over our competitors. The more I thought about that possibility the more my skepticism waned.

Dr. Richie sent me a confidential copy of the personality test that afternoon, with the assurance that the details of the study would follow within a week. Immediately, of course, I took the test myself. Before I reveal my score, I'd like you to take the test yourself so you can see the results first–hand.

Of the four geometric symbols listed below, pick the one that you feel best describes your personality. Read on to discover what that symbol reveals about you. Take no more than seven seconds to make your decision. Remember, as with all multiple choice tests, your first choice is usually the right choice. Take the test now.

Which symbol best characterizes your personality?

Fig.1
Personality Symbols

[Square]: If you selected the square, our industrial psychologists say that you exemplify unusual intelligence. Squares often are the smartest people in an organization, usually exhibiting a strong desire and ability to solve complex problems. (Suddenly everybody wants to be a square, huh?)

[Triangle]: These people tend to be the most aggressive, whatever the situation. Stay on the lookout for triangles, since they can generally be depended upon picking up the check. When in the company of triangles, however, make sure they don't pick up your paycheck as well!

[Circle]: According to our industrial psychologists, those who select the circle as the geometric symbol that best describes their personality have a strong penchant for leadership. If you happen to be a circle who does not yet own your own company, you'll undoubtedly be taking one over shortly.

[Star]: For some strange reason, this symbol seems a favorite choice among business people. Stars, the test claims, have a propensity for sex, booze and gambling. This may explain why some stars seem to be less than alert once the sun comes up in the morning.

After taking the test, I became a firm believer . . . especially since I chose the square. (Really, I did). For a week I tested all my friends, relatives, and customers, boasting to them that I was among the few chosen squares. As it turned out, the square actually symbolized "blockhead" because a week later Dr. Richie sent me the study's "details":

> *Dear Bob,*
> *We at the Marketing Research Division would like to thank you for introducing a bit of fun into our department. Before you start framing your office with pictures of squares and sending your sales-people out in the field with cookie cutters, I should tell you that we've been having a pretty good laugh at your expense. That "confidential" study is a hoax! Honestly, Bob, did you really think that some magic test could show you the truth about yourself and others? Thanks for the laughs. Hope there's no hard feelings,*
>
> *Dr. Dick Richie*

So the good doctor got me, and maybe he got you, too. I was a little embarrassed, but I did learn this valuable lesson from the experience:

There are no short-cuts to success.

Also, I learned that industrial psychologists have too much time on their hands.

LOOKING FOR ANSWERS IN ALL THE WRONG PLACES

Although the personality test did not provide a magic formula for success, it taught me something crucial about the subject. Above all, it made me ask important questions: Why was I so quick to put my suspicions aside? What made me abandon my healthy skepticism? What made the personality test so enticing?

Perhaps I ignored my suspicions because I wanted to achieve the big rewards the test seemed to promise. The idea of being able to read strangers as quickly as a comic book is certainly appealing to anyone in sales. I believe, however, more was going on than simply my desire for professional success.

When testing myself, I trusted those symbols to reveal something about me. Since knowing one's self can seem much more difficult than knowing others, I was enticed by not only the promise of understanding my customers but the hope of finding that key to knowing myself.

We know there's no easy way to arrive at the ultimate truth about ourselves or others, yet part of us remains vulnerable to the promise of one magic formula or trendy trick that can instantly tell all. Horoscopes, palm readings, Tarot cards and psychic phone-lines attest to our willingness to go to supernatural lengths to penetrate the mysteries of our world and ourselves. To some degree, we believe that if we could find one quick key to unlocking life's great mysteries, we just might attain ultimate success.

As the personality test hoax made clear, the bad news is that there's no key, no trick, no magic formula waiting to be stumbled upon. The only surefire way to gain an edge on the competition is to recognize that there is no surefire way. The good news, however, is that certain systems of thought can guide us to the knowledge we crave and the success we deserve.

With time and direction, we can gain an edge on the competition and ultimately gain greater control over our own happiness. Believe it:

There's no magic formula for success, but there are reliable principles.

The reliable principles I want to share with you are the ones recreated in this book; such classic human wisdom, of course, has existed for centuries between the covers of Homer's Odyssey. It isn't magical, it isn't instantaneous, and it certainly isn't as easy as deciding between a circle and a square. But it can enhance the level of success you achieve in your life.

Despite our temporary preoccupation with magic formulas, we have not really strayed outside the bounds of The Managerial Odyssey. Our plights as heroes of diverse odysseys in the mid–1990s are strikingly similar to that of Odysseus in the eighth century B.C. Just as Homer's hero wanders throughout his journey, we strayed a little from the path in the hopes of finding a short–cut.

Like the distractions that tempted Odysseus off his path, our temporary distraction ultimately proves beneficial. Besides calling attention to our desire for greater knowledge and success, our straying has alerted us to our vulnerability to false temptations.

It's time now to eschew the quick and (seemingly) easy path to success and accept the challenge of the longer—perhaps more arduous—but true direction. This is an odyssey, after all.

The three keys to success that Odysseus discovered over two thousand years ago make up the three major sections of this book. As Odysseus learned, to find success he must:

- Rediscover who he is

- Convince others to help him on his road to success

- Demonstrate that he is a good leader.

These three central principles of the Odyssey are fundamental demonstrations of how and why *The Managerial Odyssey* can help you become a success. They are neither quick nor easy, but they can help us achieve a heroic homecoming.

LAUGHING ALL THE WAY HOME

Before we get underway, there's another important discovery to make. As I hope you've already noticed, this book pulses with a sense of fun. What else did our personality test teach us, after all, if not that we can learn from our mistakes and still have a good time? In fact, the most valuable lesson I learned from that experience—and one I will share with you throughout—is that having fun is a basic ingredient for any good formula for success.

That's why, if we're to make real changes in attitudes and actions, we first must commit to enjoying the process of change. Do you consider having fun an important part of life? Is having fun on the job an important part of business?

If you answered "no" to either of these questions, please read on. If, on the other hand, you believe having fun is an important part of your life and our workaday world, you still need to read on. I'll prove you need to believe in having even more fun. As we'll soon see, more fun equates with more success.

Section I:
Three Rules for the Road

Your journey then will be no vain thing nor go unaccomplished . . .
And that journey for which you are so urgent will not be long now,
such a companion am I to you, as of your father. I will fit you out a
fast ship; I myself will go with you.

—Book One of Homer's Odyssey

Chapter One:

ALL WORK AND NO PLAY. . . (MAKES LIFE A DULL BORE)

Most of us don't really believe that having fun is essential to success. We know we should enjoy our work, but still many of us grump, gripe, and grimace our way from nine-to-five every day (not to mention after-hours complaining that goes on with sympathetic family and friends). We know it's absurd, tiring, and just plain wrong to hate, dislike, or merely tolerate what we do. We understand the basic premise of having fun, but for some reason we can't seem to apply it to our lives.

So how do we break the pattern? How do we put an end to the downward spiral of unhappiness?

In my business experiences, I've found three keys to unlocking the problem of job dissatisfaction—keys which can also open the door to unlimited success in business and the rest of life.

Chapters One, Two, and Three explore these fascinating keys in detail. Each of these keys is expressed by an easily remembered rule. We begin with perhaps the most important one. As you've probably already guessed,

Rule #1: You have to have fun to become successful!

I can't stress enough the seriousness of the first rule of fun. It may sound trite and you may have heard it before, but there's truth to the saying, "if you're not having fun, the job's not getting done"— not to the satisfaction of your business, your clients, your people, or yourself. If you're not having fun, chances are your co-workers aren't happy, chances are your customers aren't happy, and undoubtedly, you aren't happy either. That's a problem: not just an attitude problem or a personality problem, but a *business* problem.

Since we spend at least half our waking lives on the job, we ought to like what we do. Fun on the job, in fact, ought to be a precondition for our careers. Whether you work within or help create a working environment, that environment simply must be a place where fun is not only an acceptable but an encouraged attitude on the part of the people in your organization. (See Chapter Nine for specific examples of how to create a working environment centered around the concept of fun.)

In my many travels, I've seen too many businesses—many no longer with us—that didn't take fun seriously enough. As performance studies repeatedly show, the absence of play, creativity, and camaraderie is the most dominant characteristic of a poorly performing team. The question: How do we change our attitudes and environments to make them conducive to happiness, satisfaction, and just plain fun?

WHEN IS MOTIVATION AN EFFECTIVE MOTIVATOR?

A lot of books promise to increase job satisfaction with motivational techniques. They claim that once we learn to reward, empower, or motivate our employees (or our children, our pets and our in–laws) with the right external stimulus—be it praise, recognition or a raise—our world will become a better place. At the risk of alienating certain publishers, I must tell you not to waste your time or money on these books.

Experience teaches us that motivational techniques work neither consistently nor over the long run. Such techniques can't sustain job satisfaction because people always want more. And when they get more, they want more. And when you give them more, they still want more! Those of us with children well understand the phenomenon I call the "More, More, More Effect." Because of the nature of human beings, no stimulus ever provides sufficient motivation for very long.

Take money, for example. While many consider money the greatest motivator of all, I find it especially vulnerable to the "More, More, More Effect." Money creates a never-ending chain of desire that it ultimately can never satisfy. The 1994-95 baseball strike certainly proves this point. Though a world war could not stop American baseball, the desire for More, More, More money could. Because millionaires could not agree with billionaires, the rest of us poor slobs lost our national pastime. You tell me: Is money a good motivator?

No sooner do we get a raise, bonus or a lottery windfall, invariably most of us want more. In fact, we feel we need more just to attain the same level of satisfaction we felt when we got our last raise!

"More, More, More" operates on the same level as physical hunger. External motivators, like food, satisfy only temporarily; no matter how much we eat today, our desire for food will have us back at the trough tomorrow. The food in the trough is irrelevant. What matters is hunger itself, an inner desire only satisfied by something outside.

In my first dozen years as a team leader I experimented with various motivational techniques, with limited success. When I gave my people more money, they soon wanted even more; unless they got it, their motivation suffered. Additional money helped for a while, but never sustained job satisfaction for long.

The same went for other motivational stimuli. My people wanted praise. I gave them praise. They wanted promotions. I gave them promotions. They wanted recognition and awards. I gave them these, too. But still they wanted more, more, more. Despite my best efforts, my people were depressed, unmotivated and worried about 350 days of the year instead of 365.

If you want to motivate someone for an afternoon or for the duration of a short project, then by all means, try an external motivator—a bonus, added recognition, whatever. But if you want to keep them truly motivated throughout the year, you need to look elsewhere. In other words,

Don't count on short-term motivators to provide long-term satisfaction.

Experience also teaches us that only self-motivators can maintain job satisfaction. External reward systems ultimately prove disappointing because they can't keep us satisfied or motivated. To put it another way, the problem with the proverbial carrot on a stick is that eventually the driver runs out of carrots or the horse gets tired of the chase. Internal reward systems, however, guide that human desire for more, more, more in more constructive ways. As keeper of the carrots, you distribute your own rewards. No longer at the mercy of bosses or their budgets, you oversee your own job satisfaction and decide to enjoy what you do—sure sounds like fun to me!

The achievement of internal rewards requires that you, as the famed Greek dictum states, "know thyself." That knowledge begins with a thorough questioning of your present work situation and your future goals. Ask yourself these important questions:

- What must you do to feel good about yourself at the end of the day? By the end of each work week?

- What must you accomplish before you retire?

- What areas can you improve to feel more complete?

- What *don't* you need to accomplish?

- How can you be more efficient with your time?

- How can you mark your progress—daily, weekly, month-ly—so you know you're on track with your goals. Not your bosses' goals or organizations' goals, but your own?

Long-term job satisfaction must be linked to lifetime goals. If you spend half of your waking hours on the job, it's not unreasonable to expect to meet half of those goals in the office. Find your motivation in those things that do not merely get you from step-to-step or day-to-day, but up the entire mountain. If you manage people, it makes sense to help them do the same. By helping others you transform your leadership style from that of a manager to a mentor, from teller to a teacher. In the end, you'll enjoy your work relationships better . . . and so will your people.

THE TOP FIVE DE-MOTIVATORS

I know, I know. Self–motivation sounds good in theory, but in practice you know that as long as going to work means— fill in the blank— you won't be blissfully chomping on carrots at the top of any mountain. You know as long as there's —fill in the blank—, the office will be the place to frustrate, not achieve, your life's goals.

A de-motivator is a term I use for those "fill in the blanks" that stand between us and job satisfaction. Listing our own personal de-motivators can be illuminating, so here's another short exercise. Take a second and jot down the top five things that de-motivate you on the job. What gets you down? Impedes your progress? Prevents you from having fun at work? (If you can't limit yourself to a mere five, feel free to use the margins, the front cover, the back cover, the bookmark, the receipt, . . .)

1. _____

2. _____

3. _____

4. _____

5. _____

When I put the same question to my sales people, their top five de-motivators were (in no particular order):

- my boss

- my product

- the product price

- my team

- red tape

Though their responses pertain to sales, my experience with business seminar attendees from all walks of life confirms these to be the most common offenders for us all. (As for that first "boss" item, they didn't mean me, of course. They were referring to their direct level management . . . or so they told me at the time).

Seriously, I can't tell you how many times I've heard my sales people complain:

- "My boss! My boss de-motivates me! If only I had a decent boss who actually helped me get the job done, then, then I'd be successful!"

- "The product is lousy! If only I had a better, more interesting product to work with, then I'd love this job!"

- "The price! I have a great product, but the darn price is too high. If I could just give it away, my job would be so much easier!"

- "Bob, you should see the dunces I have to work with! Incompetent. Inflexible. Miserable. If only I were on the right team, then I'd finally get somewhere."

- "My Gosh! The bureaucracy! My job has so many layers of red tape you can't go to the bathroom without sticking to something!"

(*Note: The first three are typical complaints of sales people. After 25-plus years in sales, I have finally determined what sales people fantasize about most: a great boss, a product that's easy to sell—if not free—and a large salary for their troubles.)

Whatever the management level, I've found that de-motivators are remarkably similar. If you're a team leader, you can begin to address these de-motivators in two ways.

First, ask your people to make a list of those things that disappoint, frustrate, and worry them on the job. How many items on your own list do you think they'll duplicate? I think you'll find that you and your associates are considerably more alike than different.

Second, as a leader, take an honest look at yourself. You can alleviate de-motivation simply by making sure you aren't part of the problem. In other words,

Don't *you* be the source of de-motivation in your company.

I've seen too many businesses where the boss or team leader actually *creates* most of the de-motivators. The primary problem I've found is that we as team leaders unconsciously violate the Golden Rule all the time.

"Quota! Quota! Quota!"

We don't like feeling intimidated by our bosses, but we ourselves intimidate the bejeebas out of our people. We resent it when the company takes priority over our health but drive our people to the stress bin. We want job security, but we tell our sales force that if they don't make quota, we're gonna fire them.

So what should you do if you're one of the offenders? Stop doing it! Quit it—hopefully before your people quit on you.

Remember, de-motivating bosses rank as the single greatest cause of turnover in business today. How expensive is turnover in your business? When calculating the costs of turnover, you must consider more than just the standard replacement costs of recruiting, selecting, hiring and training new people.

You have to consider what I call "lost opportunity costs" as well.

Consider, for example, customer satisfaction. Did the person who quit have good rapport with his customers? Will those customers contemplate quitting you, too? Now add the cost of inexperienced new people. No matter how gifted a new hire may be, she still requires time to go up the learning curve. How long will it take this new person to reach the same level of expertise as the one who left the job?

Finally, consider the stress factor. An entire team will feel the loss of even one individual. Worse, quitting or firing places an undo amount of stress on the rest of the organization. When a team member leaves, consciously or unconsciously everyone wonders: who's next?

Team leaders must take control of their business environments. As with all unhealthy patterns of behavior, the cycle of abuse will continue to turn round and round only as long as those in charge keep spinning the wheel. Put an end to unhealthy relationships by showing your people the same respect, consideration, and camaraderie that you desire from your superiors.

Since we all learn by imitation, make a mental note of the ways your boss de-motivates you, then resolve never to pass that destructive behavior on down the line. Remember, like you, your people need to have fun to become successful.

BIG-TIME DE-MOTIVATORS

Unfortunately, it isn't always easy to find clear–cut ways to eliminate de-motivators. Usually, things apt to threaten job satisfaction—the boss, the product, the price, the team, and red tape—exist well outside our realm of control. The very fact that we can't do anything about them only heightens our frustration level.

How many of the de-motivators can you really change? Aside from just flat out quitting your job, can you change your boss? Can you improve the product? What about product price or your organization's money management? Can you make needed changes to your team? Or reduce red tape?

I suspect that while you can have an impact on some of these problems, realistically you cannot expect to fix them all. And even in those rare moments when we do feel like we have it all under control, another problem creeps up, then another—ad nauseam.

Despite your level of frustration and your best intentions, you simply cannot master those things beyond your control. You can't. I can't. No one can. In fact, if you have no control over de-motivators, why worry about them? Learn not to worry about things beyond your control. When you really can't do anything about it, admit it, and then move on.

We accomplish nothing in a de-motivated state of mind. Indeed, if we allow anything beyond our control to dominate us, we effectively doom ourselves to the negative thought of de-motivation and severely impede our chances of ever accomplishing anything positive.

Perhaps you want to hang on to your worries, and you're still not fully committed to rule #1 *(You have to have fun to become successful)*. Consider, then, this real life example. In 1983 AT&T underwent some "minor" (as in the key used in funeral marches) changes called divestiture. With the break up of the Bell system, AT&T was forced by the courts to divest itself of eighty billion dollars in assets, which created a tidal wave of anxiety throughout all levels of the company.

To make matters worse, at that time I was responsible for selling two business telephone systems: Horizon VS and Horizon B. Bearing in mind that I work for the technological communications giant of the free world, can you guess what VS and B stood for? Video Systems? Virtual Sonorousness? Veritable Somnambulism? Unfortunately, none of the above. The VS stood for V-e-r-y / S-m-a-l-l —and yes, you guessed it, the B stood for B-i-g. So let me sum this up: the year we divested ourselves of eighty billion in assets, I was out selling "Very Small" and "Big" products as the flagship vehicles of our company, and I was told to succeed. Are we having fun yet?

Despite enormous potential for complete and utter de-motivation, my sales force and I managed to have fun; consequently, we met with success. In fact, we finished the year at 173 percent of our sales objectives; and I, your humble author, was named Top Branch Manager for 1983.

How did we succeed in the midst of so many probable de-motivators? I didn't allow myself or my team members to focus attention on situations beyond our control. My people sold very small and big products, admittedly outdated at the time, but I simply would not allow them to dwell on the negatives. They had a difficult quota, but I wouldn't let them worry about that either. We were successful because we focused on selling the product at hand and not on the negatives that surrounded us.

I told them then and I challenge you now: don't let anything beyond your control keep you down. If you believe having fun is truly a prerequisite to success, stop worrying!

THE GLASS IS ALWAYS HALF FULL

I am repeatedly amazed at how difficult it is for some of us not to worry. We Westerners have a history of dwelling on the negative, it seems. Consider, for example, these infamous predictions, quoted from *The Experts Speak* by Christopher Power (New York: Pantheon Books, 1984).

"That's an amazing invention, but who would ever want to use one of them?"
— Pres. Rutherford B. Hayes' thoughts on the future of the telephone in 1876.

"Playing the Russians will be a lesson in futility . . . You know what our chances are? Slim to None."
— Herb Brooks, coach of the U.S. hockey team before they won the Gold medal in 1981.

"The world will little note nor long remember what we say here."
— Abraham Lincoln before delivering Gettysburg Address, 1863.

"The boy will come to nothing."
— Jakob Freud commenting on his son's prospects after his 8-year-old son, Sigmund, relieved himself in the master bedroom, 1864.

"Don't do it . . . I've seen a sandlot team clobber him. All he'll do is take up space for two years and give the papers more ammunition to throw at you."
— Branch Rickey, advising his father not to sign Sandy Koufax, 1955.

"Women play about 25 percent as good as men . . . Women are brought up from the time they're 6 years old to read books, eat candy and go to dancing class. They can't compete against men."
— Bobby Riggs, loser to Billy Jean King, 1973.

"*Gone with the Wind* is going to be the biggest flop in Hollywood history. I'm just glad it'll be Clark Gable who's falling flat on his face and not Gary Cooper."
— Gary Cooper after turning down the role of Rhett Butler in 1938.

"I'm going to get out of this [film] business. It's too much for me. I'll never catch on. It's too fast. I can't tell what I'm doing or what anybody wants me to do."
— Charlie Chaplin, c. 1914.

If such quotes can teach us anything, it's that we are too ready to contemplate the worst in ourselves and the world around us. Unfortunately, the time spent worrying has no appreciable effect on the likelihood of catastrophe. If more anticipated despair led to less cause for actual despair, we might be on to something worthwhile!

Preoccupation with the negative only serves to make us unreasonably cautious at best, de-motivated and depressed at worst. Negative thinking becomes a self-fulfilling prophecy: We said we were going to fail, and—lo! and behold!—we did.

To eliminate de-motivating influences, we must eliminate the negatives. We must convince ourselves that most things in life, if we let them, can be turned into positive experiences. We must believe that someone might find a use for the telephone and that there's hope for a young Sigmund Freud.

Of course, we can reduce our worries without throwing caution to the wind. Taking precautions—be they making the telephone as user-friendly as possible or explaining to Sigmund that he needs to redirect his efforts—falls firmly within the realm of our control. Worries, on the other hand, de-motivate us precisely because they focus our energies on things we can't control.

Test question: When you wake up in the morning, do you have a choice whether to be motivated or de-motivated? Given such a choice, why in the world would you ever choose de-motivation? I can't recall the last time I was depressed, de-motivated and worried, and was having fun at the same time. Can you?

The good Lord only allotted us so many days on this terrestrial ball. By opting for de-motivation, we choose to throw away one of those precious few days. If you take nothing else away with you on your odyssey, accept the conviction that you begin every day of your life with three critical options:

- The choice to be motivated

- The choice to be happy

- The choice to have fun

When I was promoted in 1988, AT &T handed me a region that was a model of consistency: It was dead–last in every category. Rather than dwell on past failures or predicting future failures, I tried hard to find something positive in all of my people. (And believe me, at times the powers of my imagination were stretched to their limit.) We went from last to first in some categories, from last to second in others, and frankly, I haven't looked back since. Accentuate the positive in people, and it will be returned tenfold.

Remember, though, it begins within yourself.

Have fun.

Chapter Two:

REMEMBER HOW GOOD
YOU ARE

My commitment to fun in the work-
place has led me to experiment with a number of managerial strategies over the years.

In the beginning I tried motivational techniques. Since these
proved to be little more than quick-fixes, I searched for more long-
term solutions. Let's try an opposite approach, I reasoned. Perhaps I
couldn't motivate my people 365 days a year, but maybe I could
eliminate their de-motivators.

Alas, that approach also produced only limited success. While I
could eliminate some de-motivators to my people's benefit, unfortunately, I couldn't tackle them all.

What I discovered was a corollary to the "More More More
Effect." Like motivators such as money, recognition and rewards,
de-motivators also tap into an inexhaustible supply of needs and
desires.

Struggling to remove de-motivators was like Herakles fighting the Hydra: no sooner did I chop off one repulsive head, another one grew right back. I'd solve the problem of red tape, a bad boss, or a listless team, and another de-motivator invariably took its place.

It seemed, then, that neither motivating nor *de-* demotivating got the job done. As my employees expected me to bestow upon them yet another motivational reward or rescue them from yet another de-motivational monster, both approaches proved impossible to sustain. There simply had to be a way to help my staff take responsibility for meeting their own needs and tending to their own personal demons.

Apart from such external influences as we identified earlier, I wondered, why *do* people get depressed, de-motivated and worried? Pondering that question in 1984, I came across a truth of human nature. I decided it all seems to come down to a little matter of selective amnesia: we feel depressed, de-motivated and worried whenever we forget not only who we are, but how *good* we are.

"Victory!"

As soon as we forget about the essential qualities that got us where we are today, we feel defeated. Thus, a sense of personal satisfaction—in and out of the office—requires a second key to success. We'll find this key when we follow

Rule #2: Remember, you're better than you think you are.

Too often, we get so wrapped up in the problems, tensions and worries of the moment that we forget about the big picture. Dwelling on the negativity of the moment, we lose sight of our past achievements and the array of personal talents that produced them.

Fortunately, however, you need only to jog your memory to recall your past accomplishments. I can guarantee that you've already solved so many problems, overcome so many setbacks and triumphed over so many adversities in your lifetime that today's "crisis" pales in comparison. To overcome any challenge, never forget who you are or what you've already accomplished.

LET MEMORY BRING THE LIGHT OF OTHER DAYS

Let's jog your memory a little bit. Consider the number of problems your business or industry has faced over the last ten or fifteen years. Was your business like AT&T in 1983, forced to face divestiture? Was your company taken over in the 80s or restructured in the 90s? Did your business produce a product that failed miserably? Did your company endure bad public relations or negative public opinion? Did your competition ever seem poised to take over the whole industry?

Now consider the problems you've had to face personally over the last several years. What "divestitures," "restructuring," "failed products," "public opinion," and "competition" invaded your personal life?

As you recall such problems, also remember what has happened to them over time. Did you, your company, or your industry find solutions? What helped overcome them? What particular virtues or strengths made it possible to overcome adversity?

Most importantly, where are these gargantuan, life-threatening problems today? Those "insurmountable" problems somehow were worked out, handled, or just plain pushed aside, weren't they? They no longer pose a threat because that's how people and businesses survive. Intelligent, creative people always find ways to move forward.

Do you know the old adage: "if a business ain't growin', it's dyin'"? The same's true for us, too. Fortunately, the right frame of mind creates endless potential for growth:

Learn to build upon your experiences, and you'll always grow.

Forgetting what we've learned, experienced or accomplished, only entrenches us in a rut, doomed to make the same mistakes again and again. Learning from these experiences, however, guarantees personal growth.

The form on the next page can help you properly assess your experiences to date. In the left hand column under "Strengths," list six or seven main strengths. To identify them, think about what you've accomplished, what people like about you, what you believe you have to offer the world. For now, leave the "Virtues" and "How I Got Here" columns empty.

Now, under "How I Got Here", list traumatic personal and professional experiences you've had to endure. Think of seemingly insurmountable problems that you somehow overcame. List several such incidents or describe in detail one you consider particularly significant.

Go ahead and do that now while I hum a little background music. Hummmm, hummmm, hummmm . . .

Qualities of Me

Strengths	**How I Got Here**
1._____	_____
2._____	_____
3._____	_____
4._____	_____
5._____	_____
6._____	_____
Virtues	_____
7._____	_____
8._____	_____
9._____	_____
10._____	_____

Table 2.1

Once that's complete, return to your list under "Qualities of Me." In the three or four lines left empty under the column "virtues", list the specific strengths that helped you get through your most traumatic experiences. What abilities, skills or insights helped you survive the most trying times in your life?

When you're finished with both columns, go ahead and *rip that page out of the book.* (If you've borrowed the copy you're reading from a friend or colleague, you know by now that your cheap luck has just run out. To add insult to injury—or in this case, injury to insult, I may as well point out that the page you're missing just happens to be the most important page of this book . . .)

Now fold the paper up and place it in your purse or wallet. Whenever you find yourself feeling depressed, de-motivated and worried, take a couple of moments to look over your lists. Stop whatever you're doing, sit back and remember how good you are. Place the crisis of the moment in a more objective context (does it *really* measure up?). Think about the personal qualities you brought to problem-solving in the past. Surely your past has prepared you to handle the current crisis competently and efficiently.

Whenever you do face one of those rare problems requiring skills and insights you've not yet developed, realize it's just more material for you to build upon. Tell yourself you're just adding to that list you're carrying in your purse or wallet. When it's all over (and know that as with each and every one of your previous traumas, this one will eventually find a resolution), you'll be stronger for it— which means more prepared to handle whatever obstacles confront you in the future.

Read that piece of paper whenever you're feeling de-motivated. Remember how good you are: *take as much time as you need to feel it.* When you're back on track with Rule #2—*Remember, you're better than you think you are*—you'll be in sync with Rule #1. You'll start having fun again, perhaps even enjoying the challenge of trying times.

WHAT DO YOU MEAN FAILURE? DID YOU SEE MY LAST PAYCHECK?

Remembering how good we are doesn't mean pretending we've never failed. Believe me, I don't want you to kid yourself. We should never feel bad, however, about our past failings. Failure not only makes us human, it makes us succeed.

Sound crazy? According to statistics compiled from the 1991 Sports Almanac edited by Mike Messerole (Boston: Houghton Mifflin Co., 1991), Table 2.2 shows that these sports personalities' averages included *plenty* of failure.

Note the frequency high–priced talent fails. But no matter how many times they fail, we'd never dream of calling them *failures*. In fact, though they fail between 30 percent and 88 percent of the time, we still consider them to be tremendously successful—successful enough to earn annual salaries between half a million and whatever mind-boggling numbers Jordan's posting up these days. (Heck, Mr. Jordan wasn't happy enough with failing 50 percent of the time, so for a year he switched to a sport in which he could fail 80 percent of the time!)

To deal with frequent failure, all of these successful people regularly reorient their thinking. They learn to deal with failure quickly so that it's already behind them before their next trip to the free–throw line, the next time at bat or the next pass attempt. Bonds might say to himself, "He got me with a fastball this time, but I'll be looking fastball next time"; Jordan might think, "Next time I'll drive left to the basket"; and Montana might mumble, "That's the last pass of mine that SOB is gonna drop! Next time I'll throw to Rice!" Like these successes, we must all learn to

Make a virtue out of failure.

Dealing with failure is a fact of life, but making a virtue out of failure is what separates successful people from failures.

Table 2.2

Sports Salaries

NAME	RATE OF SUCCESS [1]	SALARY (IN MILLIONS) [3]
Michael Jordan	.526	2.1
Wayne Gretzky	.392	3.0
Will Clark	.295	3.7
Jose Canseco	.274	5.5
Joe Montana	.700	1.4
Patrick Ewing	.551	3.6
Angel Cordero	.201	12. 2 [4]
Greg Norman	.117 [2]	.830
Nancy Lopez	.160	.480

Totals:	RATE OF SUCCESS: 36%	$32.81 Million

RATE OF FAILURE: 64%

1   For you non- sport fans, these rates are calculated as a·percent of successful tries versus the total number of attempts.

2   For golfers Lopez and Norman I calculated the number of tournaments they played versus the number of tournaments they won. Kind of makes you want to take up golf, huh?

3 Excluding endorsements or other incomes outside of sport (the total earnings are too mind boggling to consider)

4 Angel didn't get all that money, but his horses (and their owners) sure did.

REMIND OTHERS TO REMEMBER HOW GOOD THEY ARE

Rule #2 works on a personal *and* a collective level. As a leader, I try to remind my people of their past successes when they seem to have forgotten how good they are or when they face failure. In fact, do you know what I do when my people make a mistake, fail to meet quota, or just plain screw up? I buy them dinner. And I don't do it just to be nice. I want my people to know that it's better to fail sometimes than to play it safe all the time. (I buy them dinner for the first mistake. If they go and repeat the same mistake the very next day I impose consequences. For more on consequences, see section #3). My point is this:

Turn a negative into a positive, and you'll teach others how to succeed.

As you know from this book's Forward, I've spoken to people from all walks of business life, lecturing to bankers, sales or manufacturing people, utilities or horticulture experts . . . you name it. It always amazes me that simply reminding others how good they are pays big dividends in *re- motivating* people to once again strive for success.

I'd like to close this chapter with a letter I received in regard to a seminar I had given to the Weight Watchers™ organization. In my lecture I had encouraged a young woman to remember how good she was. When I received this letter some months later, she returned the favor. As my father always told me, accentuate the positive in others, and others will perpetuate the positive in you.

Dec 12, 1991
Dear Stephanie,

Thank you for having Bob Focazio speak at our seminar. That day has changed my life.

I am a leader who has been on staff over 5 years. My name is Suellen Hancock.

I have been on leave of absence because I didn't think I wanted to work for Weight Watchers anymore. Some things happened in my life that contributed to that decision.

My dad died on June 23rd very suddenly of a heart attack in his sleep. My world fell apart. I didn't care about what or how much I was eating. Food was my comfort and I gained a lot of weight. There was a lot of stress in my life and I didn't want to have to worry about my weight. It wasn't important to me. In fact, I had composed a letter of resignation. But because of some very supportive friends on staff, I didn't send it in. They convinced me to take some time off instead. I went to the seminar during my leave of absence and what I heard there changed everything. Before the seminar, I couldn't figure out why I wanted to leave a job that I LOVED and was good at.

Bob Focazio answered a lot of unanswered questions for me. He made me realize that I wanted to quit because it was easier than trying. I was afraid to fail like I'd done so many times before. He made me think about how good I was and can be again.

I am returning from my leave on Mon., Dec. 16th feeling good about myself and willing to keep trying. When I return to my groups the motto in my room will be: 1) Have Fun; 2) You're better than you think you are; and 3) Learn from your failures.

Thank you, Bob Focazio. You've made a difference.

Thanks Again,
Suellen Hancock

Thank you, Suellen. You've made a difference.

Chapter Three:

TAKE A RISK !

Now that you've remembered how good you are, try to recall three more memorable moments:

- Remember the first time you were punished for disobeying your parents.

- Remember the first time you asked someone out on a date.

- Remember your first trip to Cincinnati, Ohio.

The first two remembrances will help us uncover the sense of intrigue, exploration, and adventure that lies buried within us all. Keep them in mind as you read on and I guarantee you'll discover something about yourself before we're through. As for the third one, who cares! I mean, it's only Cincinnati, for cripe's sake! There's a limit to just how much you can expect any one chapter to accommodate.

But enough remembering. Here's a hypothetical scenario. Imagine you're in a vault with three doors. One door leads to fortune and fame. Another door leads to a humiliating experience, witnessed by millions of viewers, which will make you the object of scorn and ridicule for years to come. The last door leads to the exit.

Now, you're told which door is the exit. Think about it for a second: Would you take the risk?

My guess is that most of you would take your chances. I suspect idle curiosity and the promise of reward would motivate you to go ahead and take the risk.

Thus, a third of you would have taken the risk and, lo and behold, you'd get a reward. Another third would take the risk, lose and become the butt of Letterman jokes. Such is life. But hard as it is to believe, the remainder would pick neither door; they'd choose the exit instead because they're that worried about losing. If you belong to this last group, read the next few pages very carefully.

THE DISCOMFORT ZONE

People are natural born risk–takers, I'm convinced. Spend an afternoon with a young child and you'll see the relentless curiosity in thought and action we're all born with. Unfortunately, as we get older, we grow so accustomed to the boxes containing our lives that we become increasingly uncomfortable with the idea of peering out over the top, let alone venturing outside.

As we cease to explore the unknown, our natural curiosity becomes little more than an inner voice of temptation. You've heard it before: the voice urging us to do something "crazy," out of the ordinary, like step outside that box.

We become so fearful of this voice that we formulate a million excuses for ignoring it.

- "What would people think?"

- "I've got a family to support"

- "I've been burned once too often before"

- "I would, but the timing just isn't right."

Eventually, we learn to despise, fear, and mistrust this voice of temptation, or just stop hearing it altogether. Unfortunately, as we persist in eliminating more and more risk from our

lives, we stifle important personal needs for creativity and growth. The fact of the matter is,

Risks increase our chances to grow.

Yet, no matter how confining our personal or professional box may be (or how bad the air gets inside), we still cling to familiar boundaries I call "The Discomfort Zone." In The Discomfort Zone we adjust to frightening levels of dissatisfaction and anxiety just to pre-serve what we know. We say to ourselves such things as:

- "I could really use more money, but I'm not going to lose on the market again."

- "I know I deserve that promotion, but my boss might fire me if I ask for one."

- "My gut tells me to hire this kid out of college, but I'd bet-ter play it safe and hire experience instead."

In The Discomfort Zone we too often act like a dog still limping from an age–old injury: we convince ourselves we feel a phantom pain though it healed long ago. For whatever reason, we grow attached to our limps.

Though that old wound may trap us in negative space—depres-sion, de-motivation, anxiety, whatever—we remain in The Discomfort Zone in the mistaken belief that this place, this pain, feels safe. When we find ourselves growing comfortable in The Discomfort Zone, we're overdue for the last rule:

Rule # 3: Be a risk-taker!

Sometimes you take a risk and get a reward; sometimes you don't. That's the name of the game. The trick is to not to let your past losses keep you from future winnings.

DEPARTMENT STORES, OLYMPIC GOLDS & FIRST DATES

The good news is that Rule #3 comes naturally to us. All we have to do is follow our instincts. (Now I'm not suggesting that you take foolish risks—I wouldn't suggest vacationing in Libya, for example—but a calculated risk is always a chance worth taking).

The bad news is that old habits die hard, which is why Rule #3 can be the hardest one to put into practice. But there's hope. All we have to do is:

Remember what it was like to have no fear.

To jog your memory once more, I'd like you to imagine the following three scenarios:

Scenario #1: Addio, oh my mama!

Think about how tall you were when you were three years old. If you don't remember, go to a playground full of three-year-olds and you'll see: they all tend to be about three-feet tall. Even the kids who'll eventually grow up to be NBA centers are still only about three-feet tall. So, at the age of three, we're all on an fairly even playing field. Remember back when you were three-years-old and three-feet tall. Recall the assortment of knees and bellybuttons that made up your world away from the playground. Now imagine being dragged into a department store or some other knee and belly–button ridden place you didn't want to spend time in.

"Ah, ma, I don't want to go to the stupid store," you whine, "I want to play with my friends. Why do we have to go to the stupid store, anyway?"

So you're in the stupid store, and your mother turns to you and says, "Now, little Bobba, I wantcha to stoppa compainin' and standa over der by the counter for justa one second. (I can't help the accent. That's the way my Italian mother talks, okay?)

"Now I no wantcha you to leava thisa spot right here," she adds, "You be a gooda boy, Bobba. You be a gooda boy for your poor momma and doncha move froma thisa spot while I go ona try ona new paira shoes."

"Okay momma," you say, "I'll stay right here."

As soon as your mother turned her back, what do you do? What do you do to your poor momma?—the woman who carried you for nine months and then endured the longest, most painful labor the world has ever known and then fed and bathed and clothed and diapered you each and every day of your life. Despite all she's done for you, your response to the first little favor she asks of you is what? You bolt, that's what. You're outta there! It's *addio, oh my mama.*

Why did you do that? You instinctively followed both Rule #3 and Rule #1: you took a risk and had some fun. Well, it was fun for a little while. In fact, it was all fun and games until you got caught trying to stick your tongue into the bottom step of the escalator. Before you got your tongue pinched and then your butt spanked, you not only knew how to follow Rule #1, but your unstoppable quest (well, you almost got away . . .) for excitement in the dangerous world of the department store also made you instinctively meet the criteria for Rule #3. Just ask your momma, and she'll tell you: at the age of three you had no trouble having fun or taking risks.

Scenario #2: Olympic Garage Jumping

Here's an episode from my childhood that I hope you can relate to yours. When I was seven and growing up in Westchester, N.Y., our garage was unattached and set back from the house. In fact, all of the garages in our neighborhood were the same, so that my neighbor's backyard garage nearly abutted ours.

I say nearly because the seven-foot separation and the twelve-foot drop between the two garage roofs were very important to this seven-year-old boy. Every day after school, I did what every normal (or ever–so–slightly unbalanced) child would do with such an opportunity. Confronted with that momentous challenge to my physical prowess, I jumped, of course.

Day in and day out, I jumped from the roof of our garage to the neighbor's, and then made the somewhat more impressive jump back to our garage roof. But the physical feat was only part of it (although

I'll admit, to this day it still makes my chest swell with pride). The speech that accompanied every jump went something like this:

"Ladies and Gentleman, this is it. We've come to the finals in today's Olympic event. In the first lane, we have the dark horse favorite, Bob 'The Rocket' Focazio. Some say the kid's got what it takes to win it all this year. What do you say, Howard?"

"Oh I'd say the kid's definitely got what it takes. He's got the talent and he's certainly has the crowd on his side. But the question nagging us all is: Does he have it in him to come back from the nearly crippling injury of last week's tragic fall?"

"Well it's all academic now, Howard. We'll all know in a matter of just a few seconds. The jumpers are in place. And now . . . ladies and gentleman . . . for the Olympic Garage Jumping Championship of the World . . . ready, set, go!"

You'd be amazed at how often the crowd went wild.

At seven, it seems, we still have a flair for risk–taking. In fact, at that age we not only take the risk but define the rewards according to our own elaborate terms. Indeed, our exhilarating standards were quite irrespective of the alleged "rewards" set by the outside world (our parents' tedious preoccupation with safety, for example, or our teachers' tiring obsession with grades).

Thus, at seven we certainly haven't lost sight of Rule #3 yet. And just for the record, gold medalist Bob "The Rocket" Focazio wasn't the only seven–year–old in my neighborhood who still knew how to have fun.

Scenario #3: Sha Sha Sha Sheila

Let's grow up a bit. It's six years later and I hope (constantly, desperately, insanely) that I'm about to go on my first date. I'm 13, and my four brothers and I have just polished off about 100 pounds of ravioli for dinner. Everybody cleans up afterwards except me. I've gone upstairs to take one of what will soon become three showers. I brush my teeth four times, comb my hair a dozen or so times, and wonder whether it's time I started shaving.

I wouldn't suggest that all Italians are vain or anything (although they are and I'm no exception), but we had nine mirrors in the house and I had to look good in each and every one of them before I ventured outside—or in this case, before I ventured downstairs to make *a phone call.* And just between you and me, after all this preparation, I did indeed looked good when I picked up the receiver.

Okay, so I may have been a little nervous. But I had reason to be. This wasn't just any phone call, this was THE phone call to the beautiful Sheila McManus—I'll never forget her name—a girl I wanted to date so badly that it was actually worth the time and the agony to get up the nerve to ask her out.

"Hello, uh, Sha, Sha, Sha," I stuttered, thinking to myself, "my God, my God you've forgotten her name." "Hi, um, is this Sha Sha Sha Sheila?"

"Yes?" she said.

"This is, this is . . ." This is a total idiot who can't remember his name either. "Bob," I said after a moment, "this is Bob." Attaboy, Bob, you are now the proud and confident master of your very own name.

"Bob?" she said in such a way that made me question myself uneasily. Either (a), I did indeed get my own name wrong. Hmmmmm. Think fast, "Bob Focazio. Bob Focazio." It *sounds* right. I'm almost positive that's what my name is.

Or (b), I did manage to get my name right, but she has no idea what that name is supposed to signify to her. I mean, a person could know a lot of different Bobs. Maybe she's thinking right now about a Bob she can't stand—some guy who definitely should be shaving but isn't, or one who leaves the house after checking only seven mirrors! Or maybe I just don't look like a Bob to her. She might think of me as a "Steve" or an "Alex." Should I try some other name?

I hasten to add that there's another side of the story, of course, one I've since learned from observing the complex social rituals of my teenage daughter. Sheila McManus knew I was going to call around 7:30. I know this because I know now that Sheila was plugged into The Network. For, you see, her friend had talked to a friend of one of my friends who told her to tell Sheila that I was going to call exactly at 7:30 that evening. (I sincerely believe that if we could somehow duplicate this information system, we could totally eliminate the need for fiber optics.)

So the phone rings at exactly 7:32 (two minutes late because I had found one hair out of place) and she lets it ring three times. She answers, plays it cool, pretends for a moment not to know who it is, and then kindly returns my ego to me.

"Oh, Bob," she says as sweet as can be, "how are you? How was the baseball game today?"

And by 7:33 we're having our first conversation. It goes smoothly because I could talk on the topic of sports for days and she's being nice enough to let me. Before I knew it, we'd made a date to go bowling (15¢ a game), and on the way home she (gasp!) held my hand. Yeah, baby! It was great. I took the risk and got the reward.

Thus, at 13 I hadn't lost it yet. And I hadn't lost my ability to take risks either. When do we stop taking these seemingly life–threatening risks? When do we start playing it safe all the time? And moreover, *why?*— why do we stop setting out in new directions, taking fearful plunges or risk making complete fools of ourselves?

FEAR OF FAILURE OR FEAR OF FAILURES?

Why do we stop taking risks?
I've asked this question literally hundreds of times to thousands of people. The answer I invariably receive is that we stop taking risks because we all fear failure. That answer has never satisfied me. If we failed but suffered no consequences for doing so, would we then radically alter our behavior? If no one sees me slip and fall and I don't injure myself in the process, will that fall leave a lasting impression on me? If a tree falls in the woods . . . (Oops. Strike that. Sorry, I got my notes mixed up with Philosophy 101).

Seriously, I'm convinced that it's not failure in and of itself, but rather the perceived consequences that teach us to fear stepping out of our cramped little boxes and thinking like the creative and intelligent human beings that we are.

Who, then, defines the consequences of failure? In the business world, sad to say, usually it's the boss.

If you are a boss, don't make the mistake of trapping people in a confining work environment where they fear trying out new ideas. Your team becomes far more successful in an environment where people can take risks without fearing reprisals.

As the sports salaries and success rates indicated earlier, there's nothing whatsoever wrong with failure. Here are two equations to live by:

Failure + Learning = Success

Failure – Learning = Failure

We spend too much time looking only at successes for answers. What if the answers worth finding lie in failure?

To create an environment where people are willing to take risks, consider the consequences you impose for failure. Suggestion: If one of your employees steps out of the box and fails, give that person a $25 gift certificate plus thanks for being creative. That reinforces the idea that *Failure + Learning = Success*. Now, if that same person fails in exactly the same way again tomorrow, don't hesitate to impose consequences. Why? Because *Failure – Learning = Failure*.

We shouldn't blame just bosses, however. There's a huge population out there instilling fear of consequences. That group includes those who constantly tell us what we can do, should do, and even more often, what we cannot do.

I consider these people the real failures in our society. Of course, they're no more destined to fail than you or I, nor have they failed more often than the rest of us. These people are failures simply because they've made other people's failures their life-calling.

Sadly, their ultimate life goal is to increase the size of their herd. They're not content until the world is one gigantic metropolis called Loser City.

Picture for a moment the failure's profile: with the exception of his last great risk—to make his weekly treat a Whopper instead of a Big Mac—he's given up taking chances because he's obsessed with the possibility of failure; instead of living life, he sits back reveling in his own misery and searching for new but risk–free ways to spread his misery around; his greatest fear is your success because that would

indicate the possibility of risk, growth and success—the three things his life cannot comprehend—so he does everything he can to convince you to be like him, to dwell on failure, to take fewer and fewer risks and ultimately to join the herd.

Don't join the herd. It's a grave mistake to allow someone else, especially one of these proud failures, to set our personal standards. In the herd, fear of failure is not only a way of life, it's a way of keeping other people down. There's nothing worse for failures than seeing others accomplish what they were too cowardly to attempt. Your success depends upon your ability to set your own standards and goals, for

Too often failure is defined by someone else's false standards.

A great (i.e. sports–related) story illustrates that truth. Remember an athlete named Milt Campbell? A 22-year-old sailor from Plainfield, New Jersey, Milt Campbell was the Olympic decathlon champion in 1956. To win the title of world's greatest athlete that year, he had to beat the world record holder and 1960 Olympic Decathlon champion Rafer Johnson. Johnson was such a heavy favorite among reporters that only one reporter picked Milt Campbell to win it all.

Campbell was lucky to be competing in the Melbourne, Australia Olympics. He'd hoped to qualify for the U.S. Olympic team as a hurdler but managed only to place fourth in the final try-outs. He didn't give into failure, however, but saw his setback in the hurdles as a door to another opportunity, the decathlon. As Campbell said of his failure in the hurdles, "I was stunned. But then God seemed to reach into my heart and tell me he didn't want me to compete in the hurdles, but in the decathlon."

Campbell's spirituality and sense of higher purpose in life were not lost on one reporter, who was the only one who picked Campbell to win. It was by no coincidence that this reporter was also the only one who bothered to interview Campbell before the competition. After his conversation with Campbell, however, he knew that this athlete was operating from a set of standards that was very different from all the others.

Milt Campbell is a hero of mine because he's always lived by his own high standards of excellence. Could you more easily remember Carl Lewis or Bruce Jenner? I suspect so, since they've both smiled up at you from the front of your cereal box in the mornings. Milt Campbell has never appeared on a box of Wheaties. Instead of pursuing the monetary success that typically follows gold medals, Campbell went on to work with underprivileged children. Today, he measures success by his ability to help D students become C students.

After hearing Campbell speak, I felt so moved that I decided to judge my progress exclusively by my personal set of standards. Campbell shared a story about his desire for being an Olympian even as a young man. Concerned, his parents called their minister to help persuade their son to ease up a little on his dream. They were worried that he had become too intent on attaining his goal. His probable failure, they feared, would absolutely crush him. The pastor visited the 16-year-old Campbell in his backyard.

"Milt," he said, putting his arm around the young man," I've been speaking with your parents this afternoon. And I want you to think about something. Milt, don't you think that perhaps we've set our goals a little too high?"

Milt looked up at him and said, "Reverend, with all due respect, just what do you mean by 'our'? Just because you can't be the

Olympic Decathlon champion of the world, that doesn't mean I can't. Now if you'll excuse me, sir, there's still a few hours of daylight left, and I've got some practicing to do. So could you please leave."

That must have been a tough thing to say to a man he respected, but Campbell refused to allow someone else to set his standards for him. And what would have happened had he listened? Would he have succeeded had he allowed this mentality of failure, this voice from the failure society, to cut his dreams short?

Be like Milt. Set your own standards and objectives, take the risks necessary to meet them, and ultimately you'll live the life of your dreams.

CINCINNATI, HERE WE COME

Maybe this chapter can accommodate a few memories of Cincinnati, after all. My first trip to Cincinnati was memorable because I almost lost my lunch there. You see, Cincinnati is reputed to have the world's largest roller coaster, famous for its notorious "47 clicks." This appellation designates the number of clicks that go by as you travel up the first hill: click . . . click . . . click . . . all the way up to forty-seven. That may not sound like much, but let me share with those of you who have not yet endured a full forty-seven clicks that by the time I got to click number thirty-five, I feared the chasm below was too deep even for me, the Olympic Garage Jumping champion, to jump. There I was, stuck in my seat, while the pounding of my heart grew louder with the sound of each and every one of the remaining twelve clicks.

Suddenly, it went over the top and for two seconds I was two people.

were way up here,

My head and brains

and my body and stomach

were way down here.

Although the roller coaster proceeded to travel up six more hills, through four dark tunnels, and around thirteen curves, none of this could measure up to my experience with the forty-seven clicks. And I tell you this as a matter of pride, ladies and gentlemen, for the fact of the matter is: Once you've done forty-seven clicks, you've done it all. If you could humor me for just awhile longer, consider the Cincinnati roller coaster a metaphor for life.

Looking back, would you say that in your personal and professional experiences to date, you've already done forty-seven clicks? If you've given birth to a child, I think you have; if you raised children, I think you have; if you been through divestiture and the break up of AT&T, I think you have; if you been through a divorce or you've lost your job or you had to face a death in the family, chances are you've done your forty-seven. I'd be willing to bet that at this point in your life, you have—in a sense— already done it all.

I'm certainly not suggesting that you won't encounter any more steep hills, dark tunnels, or dangerous curves, but I am suggesting that after surviving your forty-seven clicks the road ahead of you is likely to feel relatively manageable.

With those forty-seven clicks behind you, a steep hill may just feel like a gradual incline, a dark tunnel like a temporary blind spot, a dangerous curve like a bend in the road of life.

If you've weathered a personal or professional version of the forty-seven clicks, whether you made it through better than anybody else is immaterial. What does matter is that, by choice or by circumstance, you have recaptured the feeling that you had when you first bolted from your mother's hand.

Indeed, taking the risk today will help you recapture all those feelings of bolting, jumping, and perhaps even going out on that first date—and hey, that's what's really important anyway. Once you've reclaimed your ability to take risks, nobody will ever have to tell you to have fun again, and ultimately you'll know what it means not only to remember, but to know *in your heart* how good you really are.

Section II:
The Art of Business

So it is that the gods do not bestow graces in all ways on men, neither in stature nor yet in brains or eloquence; for there is a certain kind of man, less noted for beauty, but the god puts comeliness on his words, and they who look toward him are filled with joy at the sight, and he speaks to them without faltering in winning modesty, and shines among those who are gathered, and people look on him as on a god when he walks in the city.

—Book Six of Homer's Odyssey

Prologue:

Flashback to Homer's Odyssey. We find our hero Odysseus at his life's nadir. After being shipwrecked for days on the high seas, he's all washed up on a strange land's shores. Everything he ever had is gone. He's lost all his ships, men, war prizes and, most importantly, *time*. Twenty years have past—ten fighting a war and ten wandering—since he's seen home. He's also without clothes, perhaps the worst loss since he's about to meet a beautiful young princess.

Chasing after a ball, the king's daughter looks behind the bushes and, instead of the ball, finds our hairy hero covered in nothing but the brine of the sea. If the girl screams, he's done for. He could be taken as a slave or even murdered. (Talk about big-time de-motivators.)

Asking for mercy is his only chance for survival. There's a catch, however: Greek tradition says he must walk up to her, kneel down on one knee, raise one hand up to her chin and make his request. No problem for a fully dressed man, but what about a naked sailor covered in seaweed?

Great salesman that he is, Odysseus improvises. He covers himself with an olive branch and supplicates her with *words* instead of deeds; ever the masterful orator, he dresses himself in the robes of princely rhetoric.

And it works. His eloquence makes the princess forget she's talking to a buck naked Greek. She takes him to the king, where Odysseus then makes his case to the decision-maker. Once at the top, he gives the sales performance of a lifetime. Entertaining the king's court with a story of his travels, he convinces them to take him home.

Although Odysseus finds himself depressed, de-motivated and down-trodden, he still must survive. Rather than wallow in self-pity, however, he looks for help from others. He ascertains their needs and demands and then presents his case accordingly. Like all good business people, *Odysseus sells himself.*

THE ART OF SELLING

Whether you are striving in the classical world or thriving in Mainstreet, USA, the principle for success remains the same:

Those who know how to sell succeed.

Unfortunately, too many people perceive selling as an activity limited to a certain segment of the business population—which, of course, is absurd. It's time we all realized *each and every one of us sells something in this world.* Selling lies within everybody's realm of experience, regardless of job title. Whether you hawk tangible goods such as VCRs, stocks and bonds, real estate or telephones, or such intangible things as advice, management expertise, or academic knowledge, you are trying to convince somebody else to buy something from you. Therefore, if you want to master the art of business, you must first perfect the art of selling.

Take Odysseus, for example. His "sales pitch" to the Phaiakians contains all the elements of a well-conceived business transaction. First he assesses his environment. Second, he looks for ways to improve his image in the eyes of the customer, the young princess. Third, he moves past her (whom I will later call the palace guard) and makes his way all the way up to the key decision-maker, the king. There he makes his pitch to the Phaiakian company and convinces them to "buy" his story. It works, they take him home, and Odysseus closes the deal.

SUCCESSFUL SELLING

Selling will never be a science; it's an art. Like all arts, some methods are better than others. In this section, you will learn a fundamentally sound method based upon time-honored principles.

Every sales situation involves three basic components:

- The Wind-Up

- The Pitch

- The Follow-Through

Now, you may have noticed that I use the language of baseball. This is partly my feeble attempt at humor—after all, you are learning to make a sales *pitch* (geddit?)—and partly my way of making selling fun. Sure, selling's serious business, but it's also a *game*. By the end, you'll know how to play it like a pro.

If selling's not your first order of business, think of these chapters as lessons in *how to improve your competitive advantage*. In a nutshell, my method can be divided into three simple ideas relevant to everyone: preparation, organization and clarification. Certainly salespeople aren't the only folks who can improve upon these areas!

In the first section, we learned the key to our own happiness. Although that's a major step, we still aren't quite ready to *use* that key. Difficult as it might be, knowing ourselves will only get us so far. We must also learn to know *others*. No one travels this world alone, and often we need others to open the way for our success. Only then can we turn the key to happiness and unlock the buried treasure that, even now, lies silently within us all.

Chapter Four:

THE WIND-UP

$\mathbf{T}$he art of selling begins with you, not the customer. Before you pick up a phone, knock on the door, say your first hello or how-are-you, you must think the entire process through.

The salesperson always has the upper hand if she takes the time to prepare. Think about it: She can prepare her sales pitch in advance, whereas her customer can't really prepare to turn her down. Hence, preparation is the basic principle behind the art of selling:

Success begins and ends in the planning stages.

Long before you knock on the customer's door, take the time to prepare for obstacles and anticipated trouble spots that may lay ahead. The more knowledge acquired in the planning stages, the less difficult the later stages of the game will be.

As every baseball pitcher knows, you can't perfect your pitch until you first perfect your wind-up. This chapter covers the perfect mechanics of the "wind-up." There are five parts to this process, all of which involve some aspect of preparation. Only after you've put all these aspects together are you ready to throw out the first pitch.

GETTING DIRECTIONS

Preparing for a sales situation is like planning for an important party. First you have to know what kind of party it is—casual or formal? Then you have to find out who else is going to be there. What's the weather forecast for that evening? Is the party inside or outside? Will you need a jacket? How will you get there? The better you anticipate these questions, the better impression you'll make when show time comes. The same's true for sales preparation. The object is to anticipate all potential areas of conflict so that—regardless of the conditions— we can still make good impressions.

Planning to meet a customer, then, is like getting directions in advance. If we have our map ready ahead of time, we'll not only get where we're going a lot faster, but we'll undoubtedly save ourselves major headaches in the process.

I've mapped out a strategy which divides the planning stages into four major categories of assessment. Planning involves assessing the *terrain*, the *climate*, the *position* of the client and potential *obstacles* .

1) Assess the Terrain

In high school there was only one thing I hated more than French class—baseball practice. The last thing I wanted to do at three-thirty in the afternoon was chase ground balls for three or four hours. But once game day came around I saw things differently.

In practice we essentially assessed the terrain. We studied the other team's pitching staff, practiced hitting against a mock-up of their infield, and adjusted our game plan accordingly. Sure it was silly pretending that the goofy kid at shortstop—a kid who, a couple of

hours before, had been snoring loudly through fourth-period alge-
bra—was actually the All-State infielder for the Westlake
Wolverines.

Come game day, that All-State infielder may have thrown me
out once, maybe twice, but at least I knew to avoid him. "Atta boy,
Bob!" my coach yelled as I ran across home plate. "Just like we practiced, right?"

Well, yes and no, I always wanted to say. That kid in practice
didn't cover as much ground. But I got the point.

The same point holds true with sales:

Good preparation creates the best advantage.

Everything's in our hands prior to that first meeting. Precious
few situations in life afford us with such a luxury. Seize that advantage! Failure to prepare typically leads to failure. Why start at ground
zero when you don't have to?

Assessing the terrain, an important part of good preparation,
involves researching all known information about the customer.
Research these questions:

- What kind of company are you approaching?

- What obstacles stand in your way?

- What's the easiest path to least resistance?

You can check company records, personal records, even library
records. In the age of the information super highway, vast stores of
information are only a modem away. You may be able to access all
you need on the Internet, or you may be able to answer your questions with a simple phone call to the local reference librarian.

Personal details about the customer can also come in handy—
most of which you can dig up easily just by talking to someone who's
already dealt with the prospective customer. Ask such questions as,

- Is she aggressive or passive?

- Does she like to talk sports?

- Does she like art?

- Is she personable or business-only?

It doesn't really matter what you discover, just as long as you know what to expect. (If you don't know anything about the customer, you're making what's known as a cold call, the toughest sale of all with the highest failure rate.)

Finally, assessing the terrain also involves researching the competition. An important part of preparing for the customer is preparing against the competition. Like practicing for game day, you must find out as much as possible about your competition before taking the field. Read up on your competitors, ask around about them, do whatever it takes to acquire knowledge about their business practices.

Then apply what I call "The Achilles' Heel" evaluation. Analyze your competitor in terms of their strengths and their weaknesses. Be wary of their strengths, but focus on their weaknesses. In short, find their Achilles' Heel.

Then assess your own strengths and weaknesses. Determine how they match up against your foe's. Obviously, you must stay away from competitor strengths. Those areas where you're strong and they're weak, however, should become your focal points for your preparation. These ultimately constitute your strategic advantage. Zero in on these target areas, and even giant opponents will drop like flies.

2) Assess the Climate

Here's an essential truth every kid instinctively knows: Never ask your parents for money when you're already in trouble for something else. Common sense told you to assess the climate first. You asked Mom about Dad's mood. Then you racked your brain trying to remember the last time you were in trouble. (Personally, I had a One Week Rule: If I had managed to go seven days without getting yelled at, I was in a good negotiating position.) You cleaned your room, took out the garbage, and made sure Dad was snug in his EZ Chair with his slippers and his newspaper. Only then did you make your pitch.

What you knew then still holds true today. Never make a pitch until you've anticipated the conditions of the sale. Assessing the climate, the second aspect of preparation, involves ascertaining, whenever possible, the customer's attitude.

People are like the weather, always changing. Each and every day you go out there to sell, you must anticipate the sales climate. Prepare for a hostile, lukewarm or positive reactions from the customer, then tailor your sales pitch accordingly. Ask yourself,

- What kind of situation am I walking into?

- What's the general environment?

- What's the customer's attitude toward the product?

As in the case with all of these principles, assessing the climate need not only apply to sales. In any human interaction it's a good idea to look out for signs for negative or positive attitudes. (Remember your dad in his EZ Chair.)

For each and every sale, make a positive and negative value judgment about the selling environment. Obviously, a positive relationship with a customer allows a comfortable speaking tone.

But what if the customer isn't congenial? The worst thing we can do is walk into the customer's office with big smiles on our faces, only to be told, "Where's my order, you schmuck?! For the last three months all your shipments were late. Now you want to sell me another?! Fix my problem and then we'll talk."

Salespeople get trapped into bad situations because they don't know what they're walking into, which means they haven't done enough preparation. They haven't bothered to tune in on the customer forecast.

Staying in tune is especially important for dealing with existing customers. We could be calling on the nicest guy in the world, but if we miss two or three shipments, he's probably not going to be the nicest guy in the world today.

Of course, what are we to do when the shipments are late, and we've just walked into the sales equivalent of desert storm? Chances are, the flub wasn't even our fault to begin with. Someone in shipping messed up and now we've got to take the heat.

Perhaps no one understands this better than waiters and waitresses. We've all eaten at restaurants where we had to wait forty minutes for food. Although we know it's usually someone else's fault, we still take out our frustrations on the wait staff.

Good waiters and waitresses understand this, which is why they go ahead and take the blame anyway. What's more, they know instinctively that an angry customer doesn't want to be sold another high-priced cocktail.

So what do they do? They give the angry customer a drink on the house. When the late food arrives, they do everything in their power to make up for the delay, even though it wasn't their fault to begin with. They always take responsibility for their sale, regardless, because the tip's what matters in the end.

Chances are, customers remember extra effort better than long delay. In fact, a mistake gives the waitress or waiter an opportunity to make the extra effort. What could have been a disaster becomes a challenge and even a money-making opportunity.

No matter how unpredictable the customer climate may be, keep your objectives coolly in mind (even when they turn up the heat in the kitchen).

3) Assess your Position

The third part of preparation involves personal assessment. Because we appeal to the customer on the basis of value (an important concept we'll return to later), we need to assess the specific qualities of ourselves, our company, and our products. A few questions to keep in mind:

- What qualities do I bring to this sale?

- Has my company had any success with this customer or similar customers?

- How can my product help the customer?

Answering these questions helps us go into a sales situation armed with successes. While image may not be everything,

A successful image makes the most favorable impression.

Of course, we all know this. After all, how did we get our jobs in the first place? We wrote a resume. On that resume we listed, in as detailed and concise a manner as possible, every success we've ever had. Then we continued this expert piece of salesmanship in the one-on-one interview.

Amazingly, people forget this. They get the job by assessing their own position, by making a case for their own successes, and then they fall apart when they enter the day-to-day business world.

But getting a job's not much different from performing a job. Both are sales situations. (For those of you keeping score at home, do you see how many times the word "sales"applies to a given business situation?) We must make a convincing case for our product or company, just as we once made a convincing case for ourselves.

A successful image is never mere window-dressing. It's based on real facts. We must have specific information at our fingertips. If we've done our research, if we've accurately assessed our position, then there's no problem. Our successes will speak for themselves.

On the other hand, we can't simply bombard our customers with big abstract qualities that ultimately mean nothing. The customer won't be impressed by such bland statements as: "Acme's a great company. Buy from this great company."

Similarly, we can't just rely on personal charm to get by. We've accomplished nothing if we say, "Charlotte, Acme products are simply the best in the world. Trust me on this one, Charlotte. Buy these great products."

Why should Charlotte buy from us? What's in it for her company? As far as Charlotte is concerned, she's being sold a bill of goods by someone she doesn't even know.

Our value lies in the *details*. We have to tell our customer exactly why Acme is a great company. We must go in armed with real facts: "Charlotte, Acme products have serviced the Wile E. Coyote company for six years, and over that time their profits have gone up 12 1/2 percent every year. Previously the Coyote company had trouble with our competitors who missed several shipments over a period of two years. In the six years we have been doing business, we have not missed a single scheduled shipment."

See the difference? Now the Acme company's taking on a new meaning for Charlotte. In the first instance, there's still the big unknown. In the second instance, she's got some specifics to go by, and even better, specifics that are based on successes. Now we're offering her real value.

In sum, assessing our position means that we're well-informed about what we have to offer. Selling, in this respect, is like public speaking. If we're knowledgeable about our subject, we'll always get by. For instance, you'll never find a CEO who lacks listeners. He may speak in a monotone, he may simply read a paper to you, or he may have all the charisma of Al Gore on the dance floor—it doesn't matter. What he has to say is important. Not only does he know his business, but his mere presence proclaims his success. He gets by because he's got the facts on his side. And, as they say, nothing succeeds like success.

4) Assess the Obstacles

Rarely does a salesperson ever get to walk into a company unannounced and march right up to the boss. Every company has a line of defense designed to circumvent easy access to the decision-maker. This line is usually defended by a person I call the "Palace Guard."

With a little preparation, however, you can easily give this gatekeeper the slip. Force him into a position in which he can't easily turn you away. Take control of the situation by posing questions that only

*"I'd let you in to see the boss, but I know
for a fact she wouldn't like your tie."*

a select few people in the company can answer. Here's an approach I've used:

"I certainly appreciate how busy your boss is, Bill. But in order to give my presentation, I need to know your company's five-year plan. If you can give me that information, then I can match the needs of your company with what I have to offer. So, Bill, can you tell me what the five year business plan is?"

In most cases the Palace Guard will not be able to answer substantial questions. Indeed, the Palace Guard rarely can tell you what's in the budget for the new year, new equipment, or new anything. Other good questions for the Palace Guard revolve around time frames, long-term planning, or corporate direction. Once you've stumped the gatekeeper, your chances of getting to the decision-maker are markedly improved.

"Thanks, Bill," you might say, "but maybe if I can get to speak to Ms. Z for fifteen minutes then she might be able to answer these questions for me. Would that be okay?"

Just remember the Palace Guard's there to test your tenacity and perseverance. Moreover, the Palace Guard's also responsible for letting in good prospects—so why shouldn't that good prospect be yourself? If the Palace Guard doesn't let some people in, then the boss talks to no one. Prepare for the Palace Guard and you're that much closer to the throne!

OPENING REMARKS OPEN DOORS

Remember that important party a couple of pages back?

Let's say your directions are accurate, your outfit's apropos and your timing's impeccable—just late enough to be fashionable, just early enough to demonstrate your interest.

Now it's time to mingle. The worst thing you can do is swoop down on the hostess and start declaiming about yourself. Bor-ing. And rude. Instead, you must test the waters, find the party's mood and adjust your behavior accordingly. If you're a newcomer to the assembled group, the other guests will form their opinions of you almost immediately. Yet with a little preparation and poise you can make those first awkward minutes work in your favor. Your opening remarks can open the door or close it for good.

Up until now we've covered the four general principles of preparation necessary for a good sales pitch. One remains that's important enough to necessitate its own section, what I call "Opening Remarks."

Making the most of those first crucial moments of a sales encounter has three stages of preparation: planning the remarks, building rapport and setting the agenda. If we prepare adequately for the first few minutes, we're well on our way toward making a sale. The key is to get the door open and keep it open. And in this final section, I'll show you how to do just that.

1) Plan the Opening Remarks

Good preparation makes a good first impression. I really can't emphasize this enough. The only way to make sure we're getting off on the right foot with our customers is to prepare our initial appeals. Sure, planning won't guarantee a good first impression, but it sure can improve the odds. In fact, I've found that

The first ten minutes sets the tone for the rest of the relationship.

Poor salespeople don't understand this. They're too eager to get through the process, get to the decision-maker and close the deal. They push right through the opening remarks and set the wrong tone for everything that follows. Not only are such beginnings hard to overcome, they can also ruin our chances of ever making a sale. No matter how small, bad beginnings play themselves out for as long as the business relationship lasts.

When we don't plan in advance, we needlessly leave everything up to chance. Though some people can routinely beat long odds, long shots don't routinely feed the family. (I know, I know, in the last chapter I advised you to be more of a risk-taker. But I'm talking about smart risks, necessary risks; not preparing is an unnecessary risk.

Why squander a great opportunity because of carelessness? If we're not prepared to take advantage of our opportunities when they come, we're not prepared to succeed. So, prepare, prepare, prepare.

In fact, as silly as this sounds, try standing in front of a mirror and rehearsing your technique, just as an actor rehearses for a part.

You might also try starting off with the "Agreement Strategy," which attempts to get the customer to agree before they can disagree. Begin by giving an explanation of yourself and your reason for contacting the customer. This is a three-part process:

- Identify yourself and your company;

- State the reason for your call; and

- Confirm that the "contact" is correct

Ultimately, elicit as many "yes" answers from your client as you can. Once you get your customer in the habit of saying "yes," saying "no" becomes all the more difficult.

2) Build Rapport

While we're talking, we must also establish and maintain some kind of rapport with our audience. As an aid in this area, I've drawn up a list of *Rapport Builders*, which can be found in Appendix A at the end of the book.

These may come in handy any time and not just in the opening volley. It's always a good idea, for example, to use the customer's name. This immediately creates a human bond between the two of you. Of course, some opening expressions are better than others at certain times and places, so choose Rapport Builders wisely. Just ask yourself: What rapport builders am I going to have in my back pocket to make a good first impression?

Too many salespeople decide what they're going to say when they get there. My experiences have shown these same people suddenly get a case of brain drain, mouth lock, or worse, verbal diarrhea. Because they weren't prepared to speak, they started running off at the mouth.

"Then my kitty-cat looked up at me with the cutest expression, as if to say, 'I wuv you mommy.' And then..."

There's no surer way to taint a business relationship than professional sloppiness. Rapport builders immediately make us focus on the other person, instead of our trying to say something clever. Concentrating on the customer not only makes the most out of those crucial first moments, but also shows the customer the appropriate amount of professional courtesy.

3) Set the Agenda

Finally, take control of the situation. Poor or novice salespeople don't tell the customer what's going on. If we're on the phone, then we have to be honest and tell our customers exactly how much we can do by phone and how much has to be done in person. If our presentation takes 30 minutes, for example, then tell them it will take 30 minutes. Never lie. The ethics of lying aside, lying's just plain bad business. There's nothing worse than starting off a new business relationship by lying.

If a presentation takes 30 minutes, say it takes 30 minutes. Don't tell them it will take a few minutes, because here's what happens: After a few minutes, the customer's looking at her watch, rolling her eyes and sighing heavily. What has lying accomplished? For one thing, the salesperson's made an enemy. For another, he's squandered his trustworthiness for no good reason.

If the customer says she's only got 15 minutes for a 30 minute presentation, then tell her, "I'll do what I can do in 15 minutes. When can I come back for the other 15?" Once she's agreed to give us 30 minutes, we're in. And by the way, if we take only 25 then we're a hero. Why be a shyster when we can be a hero?

I call this the Good Mechanic / Bad Mechanic Syndrome. When we take our car in for an estimate, the mechanic looks at our problem, tells us roughly how much the repairs will cost, and sets a day on which we can pick up our car. But all of us have had enough experience with car mechanics to expect the worst: the repairs cost more than was expected; the car won't be ready for a couple of more days. Standard stuff.

And that explains why we get so excited when a mechanic actually lives up to his original estimate. That's a Good Mechanic. A Bad Mechanic is the kind of guy who finds a mysterious problem with your carburetor every time you bring in your car! And everyone knows the nice things we all say about Bad Mechanics.

And yet it's so easy to be a Good Mechanic; all we need do is perform the work as promised. It's that simple. Good Mechanics have the long-term in mind. They want you back as a customer, and their weapon is trust: You *will* go back if you think the guy is up front and honest.

In sum, it's you, not the customer, who must set the agenda. When we're making our opening remarks, we're proving our validity, trustworthiness and reliability as business partners. Setting the agenda makes a firm contract and informs our customers exactly what's going to happen. By sticking to that agenda, we build trust— the ultimate goal for all our opening remarks

Never be in a rush to build trust. There's an old Italian saying: "Make haste, slowly." Or as John Wooden used to tell his players, "Be quick, but don't be in a hurry." In other words, take whatever time is necessary to build that trust.

To establish trust, we must be convinced our product solves a problem for the customer (more on this in Chapter Six). If we're convinced that what we have to offer is best for the customer, then we're ready to convince her. If we don't believe in our company, our product, or ourselves, then there's nothing for the customer to buy.

Unless we learn how to perfect the art of selling, then selling becomes nothing more than a crap shoot, a game played by cons, rather than a business conducted by respectable business people. Perfect the art of selling, and you'll raise the level of your business to an art form.

Chapter Five:

THE PITCH

Perhaps more than any other pitcher in major league baseball, Nolan Ryan understood the value of preparation. Famous for his conditioning, Ryan rode a stationary bicycle for two hours *after* he'd just pitched a game.

As soon as one game was over, Ryan began to prepare for the next one. His career statistics attest to outstanding work ethic and impeccable preparatory habits (over 300 wins, seven no-hitters, a jillion strike-outs). Uncannily, Ryan retained the game's best fastball for three decades.

And yet, despite his work ethic and great ability, this future hall-of-famer's just a few games above .500 for his career. Moreover, he never won a Cy Young award.

For much of his career Ryan relied almost exclusively on his fastball—a pitch that's, fortunately, great for strike-outs and, unfortunately, also great for base hits (or worse). Not until he lost a little zip on his fastball did he finally develop his off-speed stuff, which resulted in his becoming a more effective pitcher.

Obviously, there's more to winning than just preparation and talent. Although a strike-out's a pitcher's greatest ego boost, it doesn't always equate with wins.

Consider Cy Young winners (and relative youngsters) Tom Glavine and Greg Maddux. Neither has what anyone in baseball would call overpowering stuff; neither has the greatest fastball or even the best curve. And yet each player has genuine pitching savvy. Whereas Ryan tried to overpower his hitters, Glavine and Maddux try to control theirs, enticing them to hit pitches for easy outs. After all, a strike-out and a ground-out mean the same thing to the scorekeeper. While hitters nearly always make contact against Glavine and Maddux, they rarely hit the ball into the open field.

And that's what the art of pitching's all about. The art of selling isn't much different. The trick's to control what your customer hits. The maverick salesperson who brags about his eleventh-hour expertise and his iron nerve is just another strike-out pitcher. He may have a couple of exciting last-minute sales stories to crow about, but, as a manager of salespeople, I can already tell you this guy's record: it's .500 at best. Although the strike-out salesperson's good in the clutch, he's generally inconsistent and erratic. In short, he can throw, but he can't pitch.

In stage two of the art of selling, The Pitch, we'll focus on becoming consistent, Cy Young Award-winning sales-pitchers. In the first stage, The Wind-up, we learned the basics on how to prepare for each batter. Now we're ready to put that preparation to use; now we're ready to make our pitch.

In this stage of the game the important thing is to put the ball in play. Your primary objective is to crawl inside the customer's head, find out his problems and think of solutions. Once you've read the batter, the art of sales pitching becomes simply a matter of placing the ball where the batter wants it. If you've thrown the right pitch, the customer will swing. After that, the close is as sure as a routine grounder.

FANNING THE FIRE OF DESIRE

People are driven by wants and needs. In fact, some of this century's foremost thinkers suggest the one constant force in human nature is desire. No matter what the desire—basic necessities (food, clothing, shelter, etc.), or such intangibles as prestige, power, success, and even love—all human beings search for something outside themselves to satisfy an inner need.

Although other life forms are driven similarly, we people are so diverse in our wants and needs that our specific desires are famously idiosyncratic. Indeed, our interest in other people usually depends on the quality and originality of their desires.

More than any other stage in the selling process, the sales pitch requires a deep understanding of this essential fact. Just as those with the greatest people skills are always in tune with other's wants and needs, so too are the best salespeople.

Good salespeople know how to check their egos at the door; they know how to focus on others. Whereas our own desires as salespeople are simple—we just want to make the sale—our customer's desires are complex, conflicted and elusive. After we learn to ferret them out, we then can offer ways to satiate them.

Too many so-called experts say that people only buy what they need. Need has almost nothing to do with it. When you're a customer, you don't need a salesperson to tell you to eat, sleep and seek shelter. And yet that's about all you really need. Salespeople don't exist to sell the basic necessities of life: they sell luxuries, desires, wants.

Here's an example. I happen to drive a Cadillac. Now, I don't need a Cadillac to drive the nine miles from my house to work. A Hyundai or a Yugo will accomplish the same thing. In fact, my dad's term for such contrivances was an "A-to-B Device."

"Son," he would say, "forget the flashy hood ornaments and the fuzzy dice. All you need is something to get you from point A to point B. All you need is an A-to-B Device. Preferably with good tires."

So why did I buy a Cadillac? Because I wanted the reliability, the comfort, the status —all those things associated with Cadillacs. I didn't know I wanted those things associated with owning a Cadillac until somebody convinced me of it. Somebody out there—an ad exec, a salesperson—brought out a desire in me to own a Cadillac.

There are two principles of desire every salesperson must know:

• Although people's needs are small, their desires are insatiable.

• While the necessities of life cannot be created, desires can be.

We salespeople must not only locate and direct our customers˘ desires, but we must convince our customers that we can also appease those desires. Not surprisingly, this process requires patience and persistence.

After years of coaching salespeople, I've noticed that salespeople will give up far too early in the battle to win over a customer. A novice or poor salesperson doesn't understand that new desires take time to take root. Even when they do take root, they can still remain deep underground. We must take that final step and convince our customers that it's worth their while—and their cash—to fulfill those new desires.

To do so, we must appeal to the customer's sense of value. In fact,

We convince customers to buy by converting price into value.

While every customer may say price is an issue, experience shows that 90% of the time price is not the real issue; it's usually value. Customers willingly exchange money for value. Or, to be more precise, customers willingly exchange money for something they perceive as value—and that's where the struggle to sell begins.

Not only must we tailor our sales pitch so that it fulfills one or more of our customer's desires, we must also create a perception of value. If we do, there's absolutely no reason the customer won't buy from us.

In the next five sections you'll learn to locate and direct your customers' desires. I'll give you tips on how to determine, in advance, how far you can go into the sale, and I'll even tell you when it's okay to back-off and try again later.

All of this represents the final build-up before the close, when we convert price into value. We'll cover that step in Chapter Six, but for now just remember: You can't appeal to your customer's perception of value until you know your customer's actual values. Once you've learned that, however, the rest's just a walk in the ballpark.

PLAYING WIIFM BALL

I use a homemade expression for the little pieces of information customer's provide about themselves: they're called WIIFMs. (That's pronounced "Wiff 'em," by the way). WIIFM's an acronym for "What's-In-It-For-Me?" (Now, you may be disappointed by this bit of news, but the "me" in this equation is not you, but your customer.)

Once we've completed our wind-up, we must focus all attention on the customer's wants and desires. Remember,

Every nugget of information may provide a potential WIIFM.

Listen to all information provided by the customer because it can help answer the burning question: what's in it for me, the customer? By the end of the sale, we should have stored up so many WIIFMs the sale is almost a foregone conclusion.

Now, to play WIIFM ball we must be adept especially at collecting and gathering information from your customers. Think of each WIIFM as a specially designed ball that we take with us to the pitcher's mound. All those WIIFMs constitute our bag of tricks.

The more pitches we have to throw at the batter, the better off we are. In this game, we don't want to be a one-pitch wonder like Nolan Ryan; rather, we must have a full complement of pitches especially designed to get the batter swinging.

Remember, we want the hitter to put the ball in play. And if we do the job right, during the closing stage we'll be able to field whatever the customer sends back our way. During the sales process, we gather WIIFMs, load up our bag of tricks, and think about the pitches we'll throw back at the customer come closing time. When the papers are ready to be signed, we should have supplied so many

WIIFMs that there'll be little question in the customer's mind regarding value. To sell a $10, 000 product, for example, we'll need to create at least $12,000 worth of WIIFMs in the customer's mind.

Novice or poor salespeople don't bother to create the necessary WIIFMs to make the sale. They say things like: "Buy from me because I'm a nice guy;" or "Buy from me because I work for a great company."

Such approaches fail to account for the needs of the customer; they fail to answer that burning question: "What's in it for me, the customer?" Until we supply some answers to this question, we simply won't be able to close the deal.

LOADING THE BAG

What's the best way to load the bag with WIIFMs? A WIIFM's a question, not an answer. To be blunt, ask your question and then shut up. Let customers answer for themselves.

It's that simple. The strike-out salesperson doesn't know how to pitch because he's a talker, not a listener. He simply doesn't know when to shut up. (There's an old joke among sales professionals: Samson slew 10,000 Philistines with a jaw bone of an ass. Just as many sales have been lost with the same tool.)

Too many salespeople start out with a specific question and then talk right through the space for a response. A salesperson, for instance, might ask,

"What kind of time-frame are we looking at, Ms. Owens?"
But before Ms. Owens can answer, he continues,
"What do you think? Six months? Eight months? My schedule's pretty tight in March, but April looks good. . . hmm, so yeah, a seven month time-frame would be great for me, but even so we could work something out. Unless of course it goes 12 months, but then that would probably take us into a dollar area you might not want to go in . . ."

AAARGH! The customer's already staring out the window and wondering about her next appointment.

Remember, we're there to learn the customer's wants. Why waste a data-gathering opportunity by telling the customer our wants? After all, the only thing we want is to make the sale. And if we listen closely, the customer's going to tell us exactly how.

What applies to cocktail parties also applies to sales: If we want to find out about someone—or even if we just want to sustain a conversation with someone we barely know—we just ask a few specific, leading questions and then sit back and smile.

No one likes a silence, and if we train ourselves to let that customer fill that silence, then we're halfway there.

So when we're loading the bag, follow the 80-20 rule:

Talk 20% of the time and let the customer pick up the rest.

Only when we get to the next stage, the close, do we reverse those numbers, and not until then. (Of course, by that time we should be tossing back the customer's own WIIFMs, so it's almost like the customer is in fact doing the talking!)

Ultimately, every answer the customer provides eventually becomes another ball we can drop into our bag of tricks.

Theoretically, if we let customers tell us what they want and desire, then they'll hand us their own personal WIIFMs—and our job's half-way done. By closing time we'll have a duffel bag so stuffed with balls we can afford to leave a few back at the dug-out.

FINDING THE ZONE

Every customer has their own specific way of seeing, thinking, feeling—what I call "the zone." Finding this zone requires asking the right questions and listening intently to the answers.

Our success in getting the customer to play WIIFM ball largely depends on our ability to get the customer talking. Unless we get the customers to say useful things about themselves, we're going to be stranded out there on the pitching mound holding an empty bag. And that's no fun. (In fact, that's the twilight zone.)

Getting a customer to supply WIIFMs isn't difficult. The secret's to be focused. Ask questions that directly correspond to the sales situation. In fact, a good rule of thumb is to

Ask questions about needs your product can fulfill.

If you're selling yourself in a job interview, for example, you're not going to get very far by chit-chatting with the interviewer about your Aunt Mary's bouts with halitosis. While you may indeed entertain the interviewer, he still doesn't know anything about your prowess in the field. So be specific. To the point. Focused.

Some issues come up in almost every sale. They are:

Price—Save yourself a lot of time and energy by finding out, right off the bat, how much your customer's willing to pay.

This initial figure's never set in stone, of course; it's just a starting point. But it's a useful one. If the customer comes to you, just ask her outright, "How much were you thinking of spending?" Not only will that speed things up immensely, but she'll think you're a genuine straight-shooter (which you should be anyway). If you've come to the customer, however, just ask about her current system or product that needs upgrading. Silently gauge yourself against the competition and adjust your pitch accordingly.

Requirements—Ask how exactly the customer's going to use your product. What needs will it fulfill? The more specific the answers, the better focused the sales pitch. If you're selling a phone system to a sports equipment wholesaler, for instance, you must know precisely how many people use it, how much business is done by phone, how many lines the plant needs, and so on.

Features—This is similar to "Requirements" except the focus is on the product itself. Every feature the customer mentions represents a desire you can fulfill, and the more desires you can fulfill, the higher the value of your product. Once you've gotten a sense of the kinds of things your customer might want, you can even suggest some more. Up goes the value, down goes the perceived price.

Reservations—Novice salespeople often fear that most coveted consumer right, the complaint. Yet your customer's reservations can be your most potent WIIFMs. Simply ask him what worries him about this product, what he did not like about his old model, what he would like to see in a future model, and so on. If you can calm those fears, those anxieties, then you have fulfilled one of the most pressing of human desires, the desire for security. And that can also raise the value of your product.

Time Frames—Time frames can come in handy later on. For instance, you can ask things like:

- "When do you need this product?"

- "How long do you see yourself using this system?"

- "Can you foresee the need for upgrades anytime soon?"

- "What direction is your company heading?"

- "Where do you think your company will be in a few years?"

When asking time frame questions, look for answers that somehow apply to the product you're selling. That way, when you make your pitch, you can present your product as the ready-made answer to all the customer's needs. When the customer asks, "What's in it for me?" you can pretty much say, "Everything you need!"

Cost Justifications:—Price is self-evident; value is inferred. One of the best ways to add value to your price is to include intangible, yet important, justifications for the price.

Here you can play a game of hard and soft dollars. For instance, ask a customer: "If you botch a sale, how much do you stand to lose?" The customer might say, "Well, I get $10,000 for every ACME missile launcher I sell."

That 10 grand's a hard number. If you can relate your product to this hard number, then later on you can include this number in your cost justification.

You could say, "If you lose 10 customers at 10 grand a pop,

that's $100, 000 down the toilet. Isn't that right, Mr. Coyote? Now wouldn't it make more sense to buy a $30,000 missile system than lose 100 grand?"

That's hard dollars at work.

You can also play with soft dollars. Soft dollars involve intangible things you can't really put a price on.

Ask, "What's customer goodwill worth?" Or, "If I could save two hours of your receptionist's time, how much would that be worth?" Although these aren't easily quantifiable numbers, you can quantify them in the customer's mind. The customer might say:

"I don't know, Bob, I pay my receptionist $75 a day, and some extra time might work to my benefit. But I don't know. . .Those are soft dollars."

Yeah, they're soft dollars, but you can still work from a percentage. If you can save 20% of that receptionist's time, and you can get the customer to admit to that percentage, then you can add that little WIIFM to your bag of tricks and move on. It'll be just one more thing to pitch come closing time.

PLAYING THE ZONE

Once we've got a few balls in our bags we can start using them to our advantage. Now we need to cultivate those new desires we've just discovered. This step involves a little bit more talking on our part, but not much. In a sense, we're getting our customer into the right frame of mind; we want her thinking about her desires as they relate to our product. Just as pitchers must convince batters to swing at good pitches, we must persuade our customers into thinking on our terms.

I've listed a few tried and true ways to direct customer's thinking. By no means is the list exhaustive (and if you have a few of your own, then convince me to add them to the second edition!)

Tune in on their language. Customers respond best to language they understand and words to which they're accustomed. In the South we say "coke," in the North they say "soda" and in the Mid-west they say "pop."

We've got three words for the same thing. It may sound like a silly little detail, but a Mid-westerner's probably going to feel a bit more comfortable if you try to sell him a "pop" instead of "soda." See what I mean? The art of listening's in the details.

When customers talk, listen to the language they use.

"Tom, have I got a deal for you..."

Customers think of their needs in specific words and phrases (often drawn from their own business), so when we pitch back those needs, we must pitch them in the exact same language the customer threw at us.

If you're wondering why this is important, let's skip to the close for just a moment. It's easy for me, an expert in telecommunications, to say,

"What your company needs, Ms. Owens, is on-line transfer."

Now, Ms. Owens may say to herself, "But I said I needed something to get my calls from the front-office to the back-office."

We have more than one communication problem here. The problem is, I'm talking in my terms, not hers. Instead I should keep the front and back offices in mind, since those are the terms in which she regards her problem. She thinks of rooms, not fiber-optics. She didn't say she wanted on-line transfer, she said, "I want to get my calls from the receptionist to the back office."

So what I need to say is, "We can solve your problem with on-line transfer, which will get your calls from the front office to the back office." See? I used the customer's own words. The sales pitch has been tailor-made for that customer, and the customer even told me how. All I had to do was listen closely.

As salespeople, we must be flexible in conversation. At this stage of the game, we forget about ourselves and get in sync with the customer. Use the verbs they use; pay attention to the nouns they prefer; observe the adjectives they use to describe things. Do these things and not only will you communicate effectively with your customers, but you'll make a personal connection with them as well.

Discuss their business edge. One of my favorite techniques is to get the customer talking about her competitive advantage. Just ask any customer what makes her better than her competitors and watch what happens. Your duffel bag will fill so fast you'll need a wheelbarrow to help you drag it to the pitcher's mound!

Answers to this question will tell you exactly what the customer values. Later on you can emphasize those values in your closing pitch—and you can do it in the customer's own words.

If, for example, the customer answers the "competitive advantage" question with a little speech about "superior craftsmanship" and "first-rate customer service," you know that when you make your final recommendation, you need to emphasize those exact same values:

"Just as your company, Ms. Owens, succeeds through a superior product and excellent customer service, we can offer you a quality product and fast, efficient service."

Now, you're talking the language of personal values—and, as I've said all along, fair value is always worth a fair price.

Push their hot buttons. Getting some people to talk's like drawing a breath out of a dead donkey. Sometimes igniting a little meaningful conversation requires finding customer hot buttons.

Ask "big problem" questions. Ask them about government regulations, the pitfalls of the industry, anything that might get them riled up. Everyone has his or her hot issues, and getting customers to vent them effectively coerces them to hand over a few WIIFMs.

"In your industry," you might ask, "what are the three or four things that just bother the heck out of you?"

Listen closely and you just might find out problems the customer wants solved. Thump! Another ball in your bag. Or if the customer says something that doesn't translate into your field of expertise, then wait until that person's done venting his spleen and then ask him a specific question relating to your own industry.

I always let my customers spout off for a while, just to get their tongues working; then I invite them to complain about the telephone industry in general, or about their telephone service in particular. Believe me, by the time they're done answering that question, I've got enough WIIFMs to pitch a double-header.

THE GOAL IS VICTORY, NOT PERSISTENCE

Sometimes even you, the seller, must ask the question "What's in it for me?" Our goal's making the sale. Period. Anything contrary to that goal's a waste of time. In fact,

Your time's the most valuable thing you can control.

In Chapter Four, we covered the virtue of persistence. But there's fine line between knowing when to persevere and when to get out. I've seen too many salespeople fritter away their time with people who simply will never open their wallet.

While we're preparing, asking questions and compiling our bag of tricks, we're also gauging our customer's willingness to buy. Most times we need only determine a price range, but occasionally we encounter a clean "No-Sale."

How do we know when to persist and when to cut our losses?

The warning signals are usually present from the start. Be on the look-out for:

- *The Busy Bee.* This is the person who won't give you the time of day. When someone does that to you, you're being given a hint. Take the hint.

- *The Palace Guard.* We've encountered this person before: she's the sly employee who won't transfer your call to the necessary people. Or who won't direct your letter to the required department. If you can't get past the Palace Guard, you'll never make your petition to the Queen. (Just ask Christopher Columbus. He'll back me up on this.)

- *The Take-Charge Charley.* I'm not talking here about control freaks. Take-Charge Charley's simply the guy who won't let you make your pitch the way it's supposed to be done. "Cut to the chase," he'll say, or "Send me a brochure and I'll be sure to read it." In a sense, these are just "nice" ways of dismissing you. What old Charley is really saying is, "I don't want to be sold anything, and I'm hanging up as soon as possible." So let him go. Both of you probably have better things to do anyway.

These are just some of the signals you can look for early on. Just remember to take everything in stride: nothing's personal. And anyway, let's say you persist with one of the above characters, what have you gained? A headache, probably. And in the meantime you might have made two more sales. Never forget that your time's valuable, too!

Gauge your time by *qualifying* all your accounts. "Qualification" essentially means determining which customers are most worthy of your time. Below I've listed a couple of basic questions to ask yourself that'll speed things along.

1) Can they afford to buy?

A deceptively easy question. In fact it's a tricky thing to determine because our sense of affordability is almost always different than the customer's.

Remember, part of our job is to bring the customer around to our way of thinking. When customers say they don't have enough money in the budget, we need to push them to see if there's value in the budget. If there's value allotted in the budget, then the customer qualifies for our time.

Think of "value" as a long-term pay-off—as in "nutritional value." Brussels sprouts may not taste too good to kids, but their parents can still make them vaguely aware of their health benefits. Sometimes it helps to play parent: if your customers seem wary because of a prohibitive price, pitch them on the long-term benefits of your product. If it's within their budget, then go for it. They'll eat it right up, trust me. If not, change the menu.

Like the rest of us, customers almost always feel like they're strapped for cash. Usually this translates into the mantra, "I can't afford it." Sometimes the customer is right: she may not be able to afford it.

If, during our data-gathering session, we determine the customer's price zone is lower than we're willing to pitch, then we must take the walk. On the other hand, sometimes "I can't afford it" means, "I'm not convinced yet." And that's when we stay on the mound and give it our best effort.

2) What did I learn from my preparation?

Our prep work may have qualified or disqualified an account in advance. As always, selling's far easier when we've done all the necessary preparation to qualify an account up front. (Just remember your dad in his EZ Chair.)

If at the preparation stage we're not sure about the customer, then we must initiate contact to find out if he qualifies. This requires people skills. Customers send out messages that we must read—on site, as it were.

For instance, if he lights up when his hot buttons are pushed, then clearly he wants some problems solved. That's a sale we can make. If, on the other hand, he has no hot buttons, then he probably doesn't want what we're selling. Time to separate the wheat from the chaff! No need to feed on empty calories! (My last analogy, I promise!)

Many prospective customers are floored when a salesperson walks away. Once, while assisting one of my salespeople in a sale, I surprised both my assistant and the customer by choosing to move on.

After a few moments with the president of a sizable company, I asked him if I could talk to his receptionist about the phone system.

"No, Bob," he said, "that's not necessary. I've got it all under control right here."

I patiently presented my case to him: "Now Mr. White, I know how a president handles his calls, but I can't really find out the volume of calls or how those calls go through the system unless I talk to the people in charge of the telephone traffic."

Still he refused. "Nope. You don't need to do that."

I realized I was dealing with a version of the Palace Guard—stone-faced, stubborn and determined. I felt like I was calling to him from across a moat. So, rather than waste my time, I extended my hand and said, "I appreciate your time, Mr. White, and I don't want to waste any more of it. I hope you'll consider AT&T in the future, but right now there's nothing I can do for you."

Then I nodded to my assistant, Marshall, and we walked away from the sale.

Dumbfounded, Marshall stopped me on the sidewalk and said, "Why did you do that? How could you just walk out like that?"

I stopped, thought for a moment, and said, "Marshall, you'll never sell to this guy until you talk to his receptionist and find out what the real problems are with his phone system. How're you going to create the WIIFMs necessary to sell this guy a $40, 000 phone system if he's not going to supply you with enough information to make the sale?

"Let me ask you this: Why do you think he wouldn't let us talk to the receptionist?"

"I don't know. Maybe he didn't want his people to get involved in the process."

"Exactly. He knows that if you talk to the receptionist, you're going to make some leeway. Sooner or later she'll want a better phone system, and when she does, Mr. White's going to hear about it. Plenty. But until then he sure doesn't want to put the idea into her head.

"Why? The same reason he doesn't want other people involved in the process: he doesn't want to buy a new phone system! So let's go to the next appointment."

Marshall shook his head and smiled. "Well, now we've got an hour to kill. What should we do in the meantime?"

But before I could respond he held up his hand and said, "Wait, don't tell me. We gotta prepare for the next customer!"

Know when it's time to walk away from a sale. It's a tough thing to do, especially when on commission, and especially when the customer could be a big sale. But what sense does it make to pursue a $40,000 sale if the customer's not going to buy? "Nothing," as the good King Lear once said, "will come of nothing." Besides, isn't it better to net two 8-pound bass than to pine away for the 16-pounder that got away? Qualification's all about knowing when to fish and when to cut bait. (Okay, I lied about the analogies.)

As one's experience level rises so does one's ability to make these qualifications. It's hard for rookie or poor salespeople to say no. They're the people who think that persistence always pays off.

The final word on the subject of qualification goes to victory, not persistence. There's a fine line between going after a sale five times and knowing when to get out. When I've done my homework, asked the hard questions of my client and concluded that I cannot convince her to exchange price for value, then I also know that all the persistence in the world isn't going to change anything. Persistence for the sake of persistence is rarely profitable. The seller's energy is like fire—if you don't know when to turn it off, it will burn itself out.

When I'm armed with my WIIFMs, however, and I know I'm selling the right thing for the customer, then I'm going to come back a second time, a third time, a fourth time, a fifth time—whatever it takes to close the deal. Thus, victorious pitchers know when to reach back for that little extra, but they also know when it's time to hand the ball over to someone else. On that note, let's bring on the closer . . .

Chapter Six:

THE FOLLOW-THROUGH

Nascentes morimur finisque ab origine pendet.
—Manilius, famed astronomer.

My dearly departed father, borrowing from the above quotation, was fond of advising his excuse-prone children that "the end hangs from the beginning" —an apt motto for closing out the Art of Business.

As we've said all along, the close depends upon the work done up front. Once we've perfected The Wind-Up and The Pitch, The Follow-Through should be as smooth as monumental alabaster.

As much as we wish it otherwise, there are no short-cuts to the art of selling. If I were selling fitness equipment, for instance, I'd never approach a customer and say,

"Hi, my name's Bob Focazio, I see you're not in very good shape, so let me recommend to you the ACME fitness machine. . ."

Not only have I opened myself up for a monumental whack on

the head, I've artlessly cut to the chase. The customer, now self-con-science about his weight, only wants a cheap and easy solution to his problem. Now the rest of the sale becomes nothing more than an end-less struggle over price. Hence, the bad beginning has an equally poor ending.

Contrary to popular wisdom, the art of selling lies not in per-suasion but in process. Only after we've loaded the bag with a bunch of WIIFMs can we proceed to the next and final stage.

In most cases the close only involves following-through on the delivery we've already set into motion. As in the case with baseball pitching, the follow-through should take care of itself, provided our technique's correct. But we can only trust our motion once we've developed good habits in all areas of the sales game.

In this chapter, the final section of the Art of Business, I want to make sure your "form" is correct, that your timing's perfect and your delivery always brings the best pitch to the plate.

IGNOTI NULLA CUPIDO

Another favorite Italian saying of my father's was, "If you do not know a thing to exist, it can never be desired" (Okay, okay, it's a Latin saying: *Ignoti nulla cupido*). As we know, selling requires a thorough knowledge of the customer's desires. In the closing stage, we direct these desires toward our products. (And remember, I mean "product" in the broadest sense of the term; whatever you sell—be it expertise or exercise bicycles—this is your product).

Whereas in the last stage we questioned our customers to find out their business problems, worries, impediments, etc., now it's time we provided answers.

Following-through on what we've learned, we now recommend solutions to their problems. The more problems our product can solve, the more value we create in the mind of the customer. As we know, we won't make the sale unless we convert price into value. But let's modify that statement slightly:

The more value created in customers' minds, the less price matters.

Return to the ACME fitness equipment example for a second. A bad sales pitch centers on price rather than value. If I tell a customer he must get in shape, I should expect one of three replies: 1) "Get lost!"; 2) "Yeah, you're right. I ought to buy a membership to a club"; or 3) "Yeah, I think I'll buy a $12 basketball or a $29.95 Thighmaster."

The customer not only provides his own solutions, but he's also focusing (as he should) on affordable alternatives. In short, he's worrying about price. To get him thinking about value, another strategy's necessary.

As we know, our job is to find out his wants and then throw them right back at him. We might first ask a few direct questions to find out his present work-out situation. We might ask, for example, what kind of exercise he prefers. Or we could ask him if he's satisfied with his current routine (which, by the look of that boiler-maker he's sporting, he shouldn't be). To these questions, he might say he's interested in the latest technology, or he works out with Nautilus but is bored with it. He may tell us as an aside he's been taking some ribbing at the office over his weight.

When we've gathered all the information possible and listened carefully to his individual needs, then and only then are we ready to reach into our bag of tricks, grab a WIIFM or two and say:

"I have here an ACME body machine. You're looking at state-of-the-art engineering—note the precision construction—which Sport Magazine calls the 'finest workout machine in the market . . . Better made and more convenient than either Soloflex or the Nautilus alternative.' I've sold these to many business people in your field, all of whom have said that it has given them better confidence and self-esteem. It retails for $190, but today I can sell you the whole package for $70.95."

Now, we still may not sell the exercise equipment, but we have to like our chances better than the first approach. Why? Because we mixed a few WIIFMs into our pitch: We threw in a "quality" pitch, then the old "prestige-price" combination; we appealed to his need to belong, and backed up our claims with testimonials of past successes.

But most importantly, because we use examples specifically related to issues the customer deems important, our pitch sure looks sweet coming across his home plate. Although the customer may watch the pitches fly by and choose not to swing at any of them, we think at least one of them should catch his eye. The point is, if he likes just one pitch, he's going to connect and we both win.

To close the deal, then, we must demonstrate value to the customer by directing his desires. No customer knows he desires what we're selling unless we convince him value exists. As value increases in his mind, so does his desire to buy from us—and as a result, the perceived price naturally decreases.

THE W.W.P.F. PROGRAM

Sales managers love telling their salespeople to "close, close, close," yet they rarely teach them how. As a result, many salespeople confuse the "close" with the "sale." The close merely extends an ongoing sales process to its logical conclusion—it's the easiest part of the process, in fact, provided the groundwork's there. Understand the closing formula as having two stages: *Solution Development* and *The Recommendation.*

In the Solution-Development stage, we devote all our energies toward convincing the customer value exists in the sale. Put "buy, buy, buy" on the back-burner for a little bit. (Besides, we should be thinking of ourselves as problem-solvers, not sideshow barkers).

Because value's the most important issue behind every sale, we begin the close by convincing customers our product is *"Worth What Paid For."* I call this the "W.W.P.F. Program." The W.W.P.F. Program asks one burning question: Is our proposal worth what the customer's about to pay? If we answer yes, then we've done our job. We've demonstrated value.

Novice salespeople often get nervous because they worry too much about the price of the product. Price should rarely be a concern, because

Money's only an issue if we haven't demonstrated value.

Back in 1983, for example, we promoted a young woman named Janet, who was used to selling small phone systems that sold for less than $20,000. In the bigger markets, the more complicated systems went for 20 to 80 grand. The leap in price made Janet a bit nervous.

Janet came to me concerned over a $40, 000 solution to a certain car dealer's phone-system problem. So I said, "Let's take a ride over there and see about your solution." When we got there, we found that the owner was building a brand-new show room. Everywhere we looked we saw signs of construction and renovation—cement mixers, bulldozers, jack-hammers.

I suggested to Janet that we go in and talk to the general manager. "I notice you're building some show room," I said to the G.M. "Mind if I ask you what all this is going to cost?"

"Oh, geez, Bob," he said. "I'd say about 40 grand to pour the concrete, 30 for the building itself . . . all totaled, about 150 grand."

Bright gal that Janet was, her eyes lit up. She knew right then that her price was well in line with other costs. In fact, what she was proposing was a bargain. The phone system—the lifeblood of this dealer's business and a thing of infinitely more value to the customer than a spiffy new show room—was the same price as the concrete!

Almost immediately I saw the change in Janet's attitude. Now she was thinking of her solution as only costing 40 grand. Now she was thinking of offering the dealer a system W.W.P.F., ASAP! Focus all your energies on your product's worth and don't worry about price. Remember, each WIIFM in your possession satisfies a particular desire on the part of the customer, and each satisfied desire raises the value and lowers the perceived cost.

The only question now is, which WIIFM will best convince the customer that what we're selling is W.W.P.F.? Learning to grade your WIIFMs can be tricky, so I've developed a list of questions below that ensure solutions focused upon product worth.

1) Does the solution take into account customer needs?

Review the information before you. You've uncovered a number of problems and now you're returning to the customer with a solution. In your solution, you should ask yourself,

- "Does it solve a specific problem?" Only the data that you've gathered will tell you whether that's true or not.

- "Is every notable feature of the product accounted for in the price?" As I've said before, to sell a $10,000 product, you have to provide at least $12,000 worth of WIFFMs.

- "Have I adequately covered every benefit of the product?" Ask the WIIFM question once again: "What's in it for me, the customer?"

When asking these questions, you simply must adopt the customer's point of view and not your own. Always see the sale through your customers' eyes, talk their talk and tune your proposal to please their ears.

2) Have you presented alternatives?

Never go into a sale thinking in black-and-white terms. Always be prepared for gray areas and always have a back-up plan. If the customer doesn't agree with one proposed solution, try another. Present the customer with your best solution first, but realize sometimes the customer doesn't want, or cannot afford, what's best. So be ready with the next best alternative. Remind the customer what he won't get with the alternative, but tell him the alternative solves some problems as well. Most importantly, let the customer in on the development of the solution. Between the two of you, you can probably iron out the wrinkles in any deal.

3) Does your proposal set you apart from the competition?

Assume your customer knows the value of shopping around. Know your competitors and distinguish yourself from them. Always come to the sale armed with the seven "Theirs" of your competition:

- Their price

- Their product

- Their value

- Their sales record

- Their company

- Their time in the industry

- Their limitations

As Al Pacino says in *The Godfather*: "Keep your friends close, but keep your enemies closer." A good salesperson knows what the competition's up to. Although she never disparages the competition, she knows all their strengths and weaknesses and can, at the drop of a hat, enumerate them for the customer. Once again, this all goes back to preparation. If you come to the sale with a stockpile of information, you can always respond to any customer reservations.

I OBJECT!

Inevitably, we all encounter customer objections. No matter how thorough our preparation, no matter how carefully we've chosen our WIIFMs, at some point we'll face critical, hard-to-please customers who find holes in even the most air-tight proposals.

Don't panic. In fact, don't even get flustered. Here's a little secret about customer objections: most objections are a lie. Behind every objection there's a hidden agenda. When a customer's critical of your proposal, he's probably telling you he still needs convincing that the deal's W.W.P.F. In other words, he's uneasy about something in the deal and wants some more information. Find out what that something is and put his fears to rest. In Table 6.1 you'll find a handy reference tool for dealing with customer objections.

Table 6.1

Ten Rules For Objection Handling

1. Collect your thoughts.	Before responding to an objection, pause for a moment. Not only does this show the customer that you listened, but it also gives you time to formulate a response.
2. Restate Objection	Confirm that you understand the customer's real objection. Restate the objection to clarify it.
3. Ask Questions	This is how you can further clarify the objection. This also allows you to narrow down the actual issue.
4. Prepare Customer Answer	Make sure you orient your customer's thinking each time you respond to an objection. For example, use a conditional phrase: "If I could do X . . . would you then . . . ?"
5. Answer Truthfully	Always deal straight. No exceptions.
6. Never Disparage Competition	No one wins in a mud-slinging contest. All you get is mud on you. Instead, stress the positive benefits of your product.
7. Never Disparage Customer	Always try to see the situation through the customer's eyes. Keep your emotions out of the equation.
8. Stress A Benefit	After the objection's addressed, stress another benefit that reduces or erases the objection.
9. Acknowledge the Objection	If the objection is indeed valid, acknowledge it, then stress other benefits of your proposal. You can sometimes offset a weakness with additional strengths.
10. Relax	An open and confident attitude will create trust and make the customer more receptive to you.

Although these rules require thinking fast on our feet, most objections can be anticipated. Say, for example, the customer objects to our proposal with the old stand-by, "Well, your competitor says he can do it cheaper." Typically, such objections are easily diffused. The way I'd respond is:

"You're right. My competition can do some things cheaper, but he can't do everything I can do for a lower price. He can't give you X and Y and Z, for example. If you want to do without X, Y and Z, then we can start looking at alternatives. But I think you'll find that my price is more than worth the value you're getting."

Then I might add, "And anyway, you're getting me. If you look at the quality and effort I have put into this sale from day one, you know I provide a quality service to my customers. I'm not saying the other companies don't also do some of these things—I don't know because I don't work for them—but I do know that I always take care of my customers."

When defending your proposal against objections, it's important not to get too defensive. Remember, you're out to develop a solution and that requires input from both you and your customer. Let the customer in on the terms of the deal, and chances are he'll not only buy from you, but he'll be happy with the deal for a long time afterward.

EASY AS ABC

It's time now for not only "The Recommendation" but one more bit of advice from ancient Tiberian shores: *Adversus solem ne loquitur,* which means literally, "Don't speak against the sun."

In other words, don't waste time debating the obvious. At this point in the game, the close should be almost anti-climactic. You should go into the last stage of the sale assuming the client intends to buy. There's no reason to oversell or, worse, to talk past the close. Don't talk against the sun. When the time's right, don't hesitate to ask for the sale.

The form for closing involves two simple steps. First, elicit an agreement from the customer. Make sure the terms of the deal are agreed upon. Tell them, "You said this" or "You said that," and then ask them if this information is correct. Get your customers nodding their heads in agreement. As we learned earlier, once they start saying yes, saying no becomes less likely.

Secondly, test the waters to see if they're ready to close. That's when your ABC's come in handy. At this stage of the game you should

Always Be Closing.

Get the customer to sign the contract, shake your hand or walk over to the cash register. When the customer's ready, you're ready. This may seem obvious, but I've seen too many sales get frittered away because salespeople talk after the close. The customer picks up the pen and a hyper-verbal salesperson keeps jabbering away. This person either prolongs the process or, even more damaging, jeopardizes the sale entirely.

I once saw one of my own salespeople blow an easy sale simply because he couldn't stop pitching. As the customer sat down to sign the papers, the salesperson blithely said, "Oh, and don't forget about call-waiting."

Upon hearing these words, the customer hesitated, looked puzzled, put down his pen and replied, "Oh, yeah. Now what's that, again? Explain to me what that entails."

By the time the explanation was over, the customer had not only rejected this extra service but had also scaled back his initial purchase. Because the salesperson didn't know when to close, he ended up reducing both the price of sale and his own commission. Again, don't talk against the sun. Get the customer to sign the contract and shut up. Determine when the customer's ready by looking for his or her buying signals.

Listed below are seven frequent signs in a sales situation:

1) *They talk as if they already have the product.* When your customers start thinking about the application of your product to their business, they are seriously considering buying.

2) *They begin to concern themselves with the paperwork.* When

they demonstrate a willingness to start working out the details of the deal, they're very close to buying.

3)*They start asking questions.* Once this happens, you can be sure that they are starting to sell themselves. In a sense, they are loading up their own WIIFM bags.

4) *There's a positive shift in their questioning style.* When the customer starts asking such questions as "Tell me again, Bob, how will this get my calls from the front-office to the back-office?", they are weighing the value of your product.

5) *The pace of their speech increases.* Often, increased pace signals an increased interest in the product.

6) *They begin to reverse roles.* This happens when the customer starts acting like the salesperson. When the customer begins telling you what a great deal this is, he or she has already been sold on the product.

7) *They're body language shifts.* Watch for obvious signs: the customer smiles; her eyes show a spark of interest; he leans forward to hear better, etc.

Finally, when you read the closing signs, follow it up! Always Be Closing. Once you get the signal, you need to set aside your WIIFM balls and head for the ball(point) pen. No pun intended. (Well, maybe just a little one). Know the type of close before you.

Table 6.2 lists these types and also offers suggestions on how to respond to each. Once you see what kind of signal the customer's giving you, the rest's just a matter of ball placement.

Table 6.2

The Seven Types of Closes

1. The Direct Close

Simply put, this is where you straight-out ask to close the deal. Ex: "May I have your order?" Very often this is the most effective technique because it represents a logical conclusion to your presentation.

2. The Assumptive Close

Sometimes you can assume the client will buy; all that remains are some last-minute details. Ex: "Okay, so I need to get the support people to call about training, right. . . ?"

3. The Minor Point Close

In this case you present your client with a choice between two minor options. Ex: "Would you prefer installation on Monday or Tuesday?" If the client chooses, he has effectively made the purchase.

4. The Testimonial Close

Name other clients who've accepted your proposal and why. This can be a very powerful close, particularly if the client knows the other person you're referencing. Reinforce this with a testimonial letter from that same client.

5. The Summary Close

Also called the "Ben Franklin Close," so named because Ben made decisions by weighing the Pros and Cons. Help your client by drawing a line down the center of a sheet of paper and list Pros and Cons. Help with the Pros and let the customer supply the Cons.

6. The Inducement Close

Occasionally you must introduce a concession or an extra "push" at the end to secure the final agreement. Always save this until the very end; give first priority to those items the customer genuinely needs.

7. The Briefcase Close

Use this close when your client wants to "think it over" before committing. Tell the client if he or she will "okay" the agreement now, you'll put the paperwork in your briefcase and leave it there over the weekend while he or she thinks it over.

Studies show that most people don't change their minds once they have tentatively committed to an agreement. Never leave without a signed contract, if you can help it. Even a Briefcase Close is better than no close at all.

Occasionally, you'll encounter a closing situation that seems a little out of kilter from the rest of the process. If this happens, don't worry. In my experience I've found that there are really only a half-dozen or so types of closes.

Of course, the best technique's not to depend on closing techniques at all. If you've done your homework, if you've acted honestly and sold ethically, your customer will buy from you anyway—not because you're a great closer, but because you're a trustworthy person.

As clichéd as it sounds, I've always found that people buy from other people. Often the quality and professionalism of the person making the pitch is the only thing that distinguishes one sale from another.

CLOSING REMARKS

At the risk of talking against the sun, I'd like to return for a moment to a concept we covered way back in Chapter 3—dealing with failure.

Sometimes even the best pitchers give up hits and lose games; sometimes even a general's best laid plans don't lead to victory; and sometimes even the best salespeople lose a sale. And yet, if we learn from our mistakes, our failures direct us to the path of success.

Don't just walk away from a lost sale. Ask the customer what you could have done better. If you've worked hard for a sale and you've acted like a professional, the customer wants to give something back to you for your efforts.

Always walk away with at least something from a sale. You'd be amazed at what other professionals can teach you if you bother to ask. Mozart, DaVinci, Shakespeare may all have been born with enormous talent—they all had great fastballs—but none of them became artists until someone taught them how. Take the time to learn from others, and you, too, may raise the level of your business to an art form.

Section III:
Mentor Management

Then the gray-eyed goddess Athene said to Odysseus: "Son of Laertes and seed of Zeus, resourceful Odysseus, hold hard, stop this quarrel in closing combat, for fear Zeus of the wide brows, son of Kronos, may be angry with you." So spoke Athene, and with happy heart he obeyed her. And pledges for the days to come, sworn by both sides, were settled by Pallas Athene, daughter of Zeus of the aegis, who had likened herself in appearance and voice to Mentor.

—The last lines of the Odyssey

Prologue:

Thomas Wolfe once wrote: "you can't go home again." Of course, we can physically return there, but we've all experienced emotionally what he means. The problem's in the returning: home may be the same as it ever was, but it feels different because we ourselves have changed.

We could rail against change and long nostalgically for days past or we can face facts: time passes and things change. Why view change negatively anyway? Hasn't our journey thus far proven that growth involves making positive changes?

In the first section, we set out changing the way we thought about ourselves. We rediscovered our best qualities and the motivation to put ourselves back on the right track.

Then, in the next section, we found the surest road to success lay in improving the way we do business with others. We used the generic example of selling as one method for learning how to improve business relationships. Along the way, we managed to raise the way we do business to the level of an art form.

Now that we've altered the way we see ourselves and others, however, where do we go from here?

It's time to return home and apply our knowledge to the workplace. In other words, with all due respect to Mr. Wolfe, we *can* return home; we can if we recognize the rich potential of making even more positive changes in our lives.

The idea of homecoming returns us to that wandering Greek, Odysseus. The last time we checked in on our hero, he'd managed to sell the Phaiakians a story for a one-way ticket home. So they brought him home and now here he is, alone on the shores of his homeland Ithake. So it's over, right? He's home, happy ending, roll the credits, grab a hanky and tell the Hollywood reporter on the way out the door you laughed til you cried. The only problem is, it ain't over yet. In fact, the *Odyssey's* only half done!

We can assume, then, there's more to Odysseus' getting home than just being there physically. Before he achieves a triumphant homecoming, he must first prove his worth.

Remember, his homeland's been without a leader for twenty years! He can't simply waltz up to his throne and say: "Hey guys, I'm home. Bow down to your long lost king." (A guy named Agamemnon tried that very approach and looked what happened to him—when he got back from the Trojan war, his wife and her lover carved him up in a bath tub!) No, Odysseus has to make up for lost time and atone for past mistakes. To win his house back, he must change the way that he's led in the past.

Odysseus used to be a maverick, a do-it-all-himself kind of boss. While this management style helped him personally survive, it didn't work too well for those whom he was supposed to lead. (Cripes! Every man who ever worked for the guy wound up dead—how good of a boss is that?)

If he's to win his house back from 101 suitors, he needs help. He must first put his ego aside (which he does by disguising himself as a beggar to test his subjects' loyalty), and then he must show a ragtag team—consisting of his teen-aged son, a lowly swineherd and an old Mentor—the way to success.

Despite the odds, Odysseus and his people win: Odysseus restores order to his home and his people are freed from the restraints of a badly run kingdom. Ultimately, Odysseus ceases his struggles and returns to being the king of a peaceful and thriving land.

But he's still not home yet. To remain king, he still has to lead better. At the very end of the poem, the gods show Odysseus how to become a leader by providing him with a model. Note the last lines of the Odyssey (quoted at the section head), which give the last word of the poem to a minor character named Mentor.

Mentor's a wise old man who leads others by acting as a good advisor, a reliable guide and a resourceful teacher. The poem's end suggests the best way for Odysseus to run his kingdom is to follow Mentor's lead. In short, to lead his people he must become more of a *mentor* and less of a *dictator.*

Not surprisingly, this ending has relevance for us business people. As managers, as leaders of people, we must follow mentor's lead as well. To do so, we must change the way we think about managing people. Like Odysseus, we have to put our egos aside, forget about being bosses and make ourselves better teachers, coaches and advisors. There's a process for accomplishing this, which I call **Mentor Management.**

Mentor Management's a method for managing people that stresses teaching over telling, learning over disciplining, and empowerment over mindless servitude. The method, as always, falls into three stages.

The first, *Chapter Seven,* examines how we might transform a boss who's a dictator, a disciplinarian, and a preacher into an advisor, a guide and a teacher. The second step, *Chapter Eight,* focuses directly on the mentor's advisee, and shows how, by concentrating on the skills of a job, a mentor can vastly improve performance. Finally, *Chapter Nine* synthesizes the other two chapters by concentrating on the environment a manager must create to help the entire organization succeed.

It's time, then, to put it all together now. It's time to teach others what we ourselves have learned in the course of our travels. Ultimately, if in the future we can look back and say we helped make our businesses better places to work in, then we can truly say we've finally made it home.

Chapter Seven:

DEBUNKING MR. DITHERS

Bad herdsman ruin their flocks.
—Book XVII of Homer's *Odyssey*

In the old days—as we Baby Boomers can attest—monetary rewards often compensated for miserable work conditions. The more we worked, the more we got paid, and that was the end of the story.

But times have changed. Money doesn't motivate today's college and high school graduates as much. Nor do these workers of tomorrow accept the "work harder or else" principle. Given the choice between a miserable employer who pays well, and a less prestigious one who treats his people with dignity and respect, the workers of the 90s opt for the latter almost every time.

The good news: the shift in the prevailing business climate actually is for the better. Why? Because the easiest way to improve productivity in business today is to improve the quality of the working environment—precisely what the workers of tomorrow are demanding. In other words,

99

Improving people improves results.

Most of us managers would be happy if we could get eight hours of work from their employees a day. But what if we could get ten hours of work from each of our employees in the same eight hour period? By improving an employee's daily output by ten to twenty percent, we effectively "add" a couple of hours of production to each work day.

Translate these numbers to the organization as a whole and imagine how rapidly your business will grow. All it take is an investment in people—truly every company's greatest asset.

When we invest in people, however, we must offer more than just monetary incentives. For one thing, such an approach costs too much. For another, it doesn't work. Not only will employees require more and more incentives as they go along (Remember the "More, More, More" effect?), but they'll regard their work as a means toward more money rather than a fulfilling end in and of itself. After all, if mere money were the key to improved productivity, then the United States government would be the most efficient organization in the country!

Instead, investing in people means investing in education. As the old saying goes, it's better to teach a man to fish than to give him a meal. That's why all the best and brightest companies in America now invest in sound mentorship programs. They recognize the inestimable value of coaching, teaching, mentoring—whatever you want to call it—for these ideas aim at improving the quality of each employee's work experience, which in turn can improve each employee's daily output.

The best asset any business could ask for is a knowledgeable employee who has a personal stake—both financial and emotional—in the success of the overall organization.

Mentor Management can produce just such an employee. When managers turn from tellers to teachers, from dictators to coaches, from managers to mentors, they've begun to make the real, meaningful changes that work to the mutual benefit of both the organization and its people. Such changes *must start from the top*. If top management is committed to improvement, then improvement inevitably spreads throughout the rest of the organization.

Before we can improve the work-force, however, we must improve our management strategy—which means turning our managers into mentors. Only then can we expect our employees to make the personal investment necessary for organizational improvement.

CESSANTE CAUSA

Sister Mary Dominiani, the nun who taught me Latin in grade school, loved to use a phrase whenever she wished to end any trouble: "Cessante causa effectus cessat." Or,

Take care of the cause and you eliminate the effect.

Now, in Latin class, this phrase usually meant I had to sit in the corner for pulling Sheila McManus' pig tails. But it applies to business as well. Put simply: to rid ourselves of bad business effects, we must first locate and eliminate their root causes.

There's no shortage of bad business effects in today's environment. For one thing, many corporations have incurred an enormous debt thanks to the 80s buyout binge, a debt that has cut a deep groove in America's R&D budgets. For another, our foreign competitors have aggressively taken over areas traditionally dominated by American industry (automobiles, computer technology, manufacturing, etc.). And finally, the traditional American worker has changed considerably; after witnessing ten years of widespread lay-offs and top-to-bottom restructurings, the typical American employee of the 90s has less corporate loyalty than in the past.

Let's stop there before we all get a migraine. What's the common denominator to all these problems? Clearly, we're witnessing the effects of short-term thinking.

For the last 30 years companies have been too short-sighted, too focused on the present, while those in the global market have shown the patience and foresight to look into the distant future and anticipate where their businesses are going.

Whereas it's not uncommon for Japanese businesses to have 30, 40, even 50-year plans, American businesses remain preoccupied with yearly, quarterly, monthly and even weekly results. Whereas Japanese savings have created an economic powerhouse with money to burn, American businesses have mortgaged their future for immediate financial gains. And whereas Japanese and European workers often stay with a company for a lifetime, American workers jump from job to job because they're used to being treated like so many interchangeable parts. This practice has produced little more than costly turnover rates and an American workforce with little or no corporate loyalty.

Granted, we may not be able to fix these problems on a large scale, but we can eliminate their root causes on corporate or managerial levels right now. We business leaders can initiate change by simply promoting long-term thinking in our organizations.

If you happen to be one of those people who demand immediate, short-term results from your employees, STOP! Immediately. A much greater pay-off lies down the road. As an entrepreneur or business leader, plan better for the future by simply investing in your people. Teach your managers how to become good coaches, teachers or mentors, and they'll develop the greatest asset in your business—your people.

THE DITHERS COMPLEX

How exactly do we turn managers into mentors? Let's begin with the old style boss, the source and substance of what I call "The Dithers Complex." If you recall, Mr. Dithers is the irascible boss in the *Blondie* comic strip, that mustached dervish who constantly beats Dagwood over the head (often with a stick) to get him going. And whenever Mr. Dithers is not around, Dagwood's sleeping on the job.

This dynamic—tyrant boss vs. lazy employee—produces the most common symptoms of the Dithers Complex. Worse, both sides perpetuate the disease by feeding off one another.

The symptoms are easy to spot. The old-style manager must always be present, stick in hand, before anything gets done. Meanwhile, since he treats his employees like children, they act like children.

"My quota's done for the month."

Worst of all, the Dithers management style is grossly counter-productive, producing one of two disastrous scenarios: a) a stressful environment that gets the "numbers" but has constant turn-over; or b) an office full of deadwood Dagwoods who never improve their performance.

In order to turn these tyrants into mentors, then, we must first cure them of The Dithers Complex. (Now I'm not just picking on the boss. Both sides are caught in an ugly dance. We'll take care of Dagwood's problem in the next chapter, but first we've got to examine what's wrong with the way Mr. Dithers is leading.)

The boss needs to learn some healthy new habits. First, entrepreneurs and business leaders must change the criteria by which they evaluate their employees. Generally speaking, today's managers (pretty much like yesterday's managers) evaluate their people solely on the basis of quantitative results. They ask questions like:

- What are your quarterly results?

- Did you make your quota?

- What's in the lower right hand corner of the balance sheet?

Such evaluations use too much math, too much cold, impersonal objectivity. What's worse, quantitative evaluations make few allowances for long-term development. Managers get so wrapped up in the numbers game—bottom lines, performance results, etc.—they forget their best weapon for achieving those numbers, their people. They must learn to pay greater attention to the human factor.

When I evaluate my mentors, I look at both quantitative and qualitative factors. The best mentor strikes a balance between the two. For example, a quantitative-only manager may get the financial results, but if he gets them by beating his people with a stick every day, his qualitative results suffer. His people quit every six months, the turnover ratio shoots sky high, and the company loses both time and money. On the other hand, the purely qualitative manager is often everybody's best pal—and little else. A good mentor must maintain her authority if she's to inspire excellence in her people; a bad mentor values approval over results.

While most managers have no problem understanding what's expected of them on the quantitative side, the qualitative half of the equation's quite a different matter. Rarely do we see a manager applauded for how well she develops her people—and that must change. In the rest of this chapter, we'll develop a qualitative criteria that transforms old-style-bosses into modern mentors.

MAKING MENTORS

As we know, a mentor is a guide, a teacher, someone who shows the way but does not (and should not) do the job alone. He teaches his advisees how to transport themselves to their destinations. To see if your company's making mentors or bolstering bosses, simply ask these questions of your management team:

- What's the longevity rate of the people working beneath each manager?

- What career advancements are available for people in the organization?

- In what way are improvements encouraged within the organization?

- How broad-based is education in the company?

- Do people learn more than what's required for their job?

- Do workers have input into their jobs?

- Do managers hire and develop new talent?

How does your management team score? Not great? Not to worry. The situation's not as serious as it may sound. By simply creating the above list, we've already made the most important step toward rapid improvement: setting clearly defined criteria. Once we establish the terms for success, we can then develop a practical plan for achieving it. In other words,

Clearly defined goals yield clear-cut results.

As we'll see in the next chapter, setting criteria also improves employees: by focusing on job skills rather than quota results, an effective manager can not only assess the potential of his employees, but he can also guide and develop those employees into a first-class work team.

For the sake of clarity, I've come up with three generic categories of managerial skills: Interpersonal Skills, Administrative Skills and Personal Skills. By examining each of these categories one-by-one, we can better understand what each skill consists of, what constitutes mastery over that skill and what's required for success. Afterward, when we put them all back together, we'll have transformed a manager into a mentor.

I. INTERPERSONAL SKILLS

First off, a manager should avoid a big ego, for big egos inevitably work against effective mentoring. (One caveat: every manager has a different style, a different way of getting the job done. We shouldn't confuse style with substance—the bottom line's their effectiveness. If she gets qualitative and quantitative results by being an aggressive mentor, then so be it).

Managers with insatiable egos often demand sole credit for a team's success. If you want it done right, they reason, then you have to do it yourself—or at least you have to make it look like you did it yourself.

Big egos like to think they can do a bigger, better, bolder, brighter job than anybody else.

Although this approach may not hinder an individual performer on the rise up the corporate ladder, an effective manager must exercise more restraint. He won't be a mentor until he learns to set his ego aside and focus on what's best for those he's supposed to guide. In fact,

A mentor puts his people first.

"That's right, hon'— right now I'm over everyone on the third floor."

An example from personal experience may perhaps better illustrate this point. In 1983, as a general manager for AT&T, I finished second in the country in sales results. It followed, then, that had I retained this same experienced team going into 1984, I would have finished even higher the following year. But in fact, at the end of 1984, I finished fourth.

What happened? Basically, I promoted five of my very top sales people to critical positions in my business, and sent several others to positions outside my specific business. As a result, I pretty much had a new crop of salespeople in 1984. Although they were good (they finished 4th out of 29, after all), I had sacrificed my shot at being #1 by promoting my winning team.

Please don't feel sorry for me: I was only doing my job as an effective mentor. I take great satisfaction every time one of my employees moves up through the ranks. In fact, my people's success just happens to be one of my main personal criterion for success.

If blind altruism isn't enough of a motivator for you, then consider what happened later on. In 1988 I was handed one of the worst regions in the country for AT&T. Yet I was able to find success anyway largely because many of those same people I promoted back in '83 were only too glad to lend me a hand.

Although I may not have received the immediate gratification of being *numero uno* in '84, my investment in my people paid dividends in '88 and continues to pay off even today. Invest in your greatest asset, and eventually you'll reap the rewards.

Good mentors, then, always look out for their people, which also means they're sensitive to their employees' needs. Moreover, good interpersonal skills depend on a degree of sensitivity.

Sensitivity doesn't require a mentor cry at sentimental movies or play the psychologist all the time. It does require, however, consideration of emotions, habits and proclivities of employees. If a mentor senses tension in the work place, it is her responsibility to locate the source of this tension and resolve it before it affects job performance.

An example: Jack and Jill are both first-rate salespeople, so much so that they both have their hearts set on the same promotion. Although Jack's a slightly better salesperson than Jill (his numbers exceed hers by a point or two), Jill has earned the respect of everyone in the office and has demonstrated real leadership potential to boot.

Thus, after much deliberation, we promote Jill. Although it's a good decision that benefits the organization, Jack's got a pretty sore crown at the moment. How's Jack going to feel working for Jill, when just recently he competed against her for the same position?

A good mentor stays sensitive to Jack's difficult position and acts accordingly. Perhaps Jack just needs reassurance. Or perhaps he wants—and deserves—an honest explanation for why he failed to get the promotion. Rather than let Jack feel slighted, we take him aside and tell him exactly what areas he needs to improve so that, next time, he'll have the promotion in the bag.

By being sensitive to Jack's situation, we've not only prevented the possibility of future conflicts (we've kept Jill from tumbling after), but we've set yet another employee on the road to improvement.

Effective interpersonal skills also require a great deal of flexibility. Good mentors know how to adjust to new challenges or changes in the work environment. In this way, a mentor must be a bit of a chameleon. He must adjust his style to suit different times, places or audiences.

To evaluate my mentors on their flexibility, I look for the number and variety of approaches they use to solve problems. By encouraging variety, we impress upon our managers the necessity of exploring alternatives. If a mentor can change his approach, he'll be better suited to deal with a given situation, especially when initial attempts to handle a problem are not effective.

Most importantly, mentors must act like mentors. They should always be measured by how effectively they influence, instruct and guide their people. Mentors should always inspire others to perform on their own—"inspire" being the operative word here.

Although a good mentor gets actively involved in her own projects, she rarely takes over. A mentor initiates ideas, asks questions, gives instructions and—most importantly—sets an example. She's careful to get input from her people and checks to see how receptive her people are to her ideas, suggestions and instructions. That's where her role ends, however. The mentor offers guidance but leaves performance up to the individual.

Inevitably, the mentor must also allow for occasional failures. Allowing failure encourages risk-taking (check out Chapter Three, if you don't believe me) and a self-motivated workforce. If a mentor hears one of her people say, "I did it," then she's done her job as a guide. Although the mentor may have committed countless hours developing the "I" who did it, she benefits in the long run because that same "I" now feels confident and self-motivated.

Mentors always guide their people in a positive direction. If they possess good interpersonal skills, they play positive roles in the career development of each employee. In fact, the best way to evaluate a manager's interpersonal skills is to assess the aptitude and motivation of the people who work for him.

In the final analysis, a manager's people are his bottom line results. That's why, when evaluating managers on their interpersonal skills, it's a good idea to ask such bottom line questions as:

- How well does the manager provide her employees the opportunity to develop to the full extent of their interests and capabilities?

- How well does the manager facilitate meaningful and successful career movement for her people?

- How well does the manager monitor and direct her employees' development?

In the next chapter, we'll learn exactly how to do these things. For right now, however, just remember: knowing your managers' deficiencies tells you exactly which areas need improvement. After all, that's the value of setting criteria in the first place.

II. ADMINISTRATIVE SKILLS

I know what you're going to say: Bo-ring. Yet there's no way to avoid this issue, for administrative skills—those attributes that allow one to organize and control an unwieldy organization—are the most crucial weapons in any effective mentor's managerial arsenal. A mentor's administrative skills are the means by which he earns and maintains his authority. No matter how intimately or successfully we relate to our employees, we accomplish nothing if our organization falls into disorganization.

Table 7.1

Administrative Skills

Skills	Criteria
Organizing	Schedules resources and personnel and develops systematic and effective means for accomplishing tasks.
Setting priorities	Correctly identifies critical tasks and ensures that they receive adequate time and resources.
Planning	Anticipates needs; avoids schedule conflicts; specifies activities; schedules resources in time to meet needs; sees that personnel and materials are available when needed.
Following up	Makes appropriate checks to see that work is correct and on time; knows the status of people, materials, plans.
Getting work done	Accomplishes tasks satisfactorily and on time.
Making decisions	Makes timely and effective decisions on the basis of available information.
Using available information.	Bases decisions on rational analysis at the time.
Anticipating the future	Thinks ahead; takes into account future needs or events which are predictable.
Recognizing interactions	Takes into account (when appropriate) other business operations.
Considering situation and alternatives	Bases decisions on the characteristics of the existing situation and, if necessary, creatively searches for alternatives.

Our people should take it for granted that their department runs smoothly, according to a set of conditions they never even have to think about. And the reason they don't have to think about it is because we've already thought about it for them.

To help establish order, see table 7.1 for a list of ten essential administrative skills and the criteria for each. Run down this list and see where you or your managers are lacking.

Entrepreneurs or managers who want to do a little self-evaluating should cater these general areas to specific, individual business concerns. Most importantly, focus intently on the specific demands of your own business, give priority to those areas that require the most attention and then look for possibilities of improvement. In sum, the best way to examine your own or your manager's administrative skills is to be good administrator yourself.

Good administrators don't ever seem to exercise their control. My mother, for instance, was an administrator of this sort: somehow my clothes got washed and cleaned each week, the house remained immaculate despite my most determined efforts and a piping hot dinner appeared all by itself each night at the dinner table. In fact, it wasn't until I was in college and on my own that I began to appreciate her administrative skills. When did she wash the clothes? How did she keep the cupboard full? And how on earth did she find the time to keep that house so clean? Her answer: "I wasa organized, my little Bobba."

Each Monday she shopped for the entire week, she kept a little wash going all the time so she was never overwhelmed, and she never, ever, let the house get so dirty that it would put her behind schedule. She followed the three main components to any successful piece of administration: planning, organization and maintenance.

The key lies in the maintaining. In the same way that we've learned the value of establishing criteria and goals, so too must we establish ground rules and schedules that keep our organizations running smoothly. My own rule of thumb goes like this:

A mentor maintains order.

If we let something slip in the schedule—we forget, say, to wash our clothes on the day we have set aside—then the rest of the schedule gets out of whack: the organization becomes a disorganization; worse, the people under our supervision start getting restless (not to mention dirty).

III. PERSONAL SKILLS

While it's still true that an effective mentor must set aside her ego, it's also true that this same effective mentor must serve as a role model for those whom she leads. As we all know, the best leaders lead by their example. Thus a good mentor inspires her people toward self-improvement by constantly trying to improve herself.

A mentor does not just lead by edict and authority; rather,

A mentor shows the way.

A mentor symbolizes success. As Mr. Maddox, my demanding but inspiring high school math teacher, once said: people rise to the level asked of them. That level is set by the leader's own example. As we parents know all too well, "Do as I say" carries much less authority than "Do as I do." The latter should be the goal of every mentor.

Good mentoring requires development of three crucial areas: communication, stability and inner work standards. First, let's examine good personal communication skills. Effective communication always requires the speaker's awareness of his audience.

Some people can pick up things quickly, while others need a little more explanation; some people have short attention spans, while others can stay focused for hours. Good communicators take into account the competing demands of their audience and tailor their rhetorical strategies accordingly.

Here are a few tips on getting your point across

- *Always take the time, in advance, to organize your ideas and information concisely, rationally and logically.* This applies whether you're talking to a roomful of salespeople or to an individual under your care. You would be surprised by how much clearer your ideas can be if you simply count to five before speaking.

- *Familiarize yourself with, and use, appropriate terminology.* Every job has its special language, its characteristic terms, so don't erode your authority simply because you can't remember the name of that thingamabob your people work on.

- *Put yourself in your own audience.* This exercise compels you to project your voice and enunciate your words clearly and crisply.

- *Use a simple style.* Connect your nouns to action verbs— that is, make Things Do Things. And in place of excessive explanations, use similes and comparisons drawn from everyday life. Complex diction and excessive wordiness only interest the person speaking. You'll make a much better impression by not trying too hard to make an impression.

- *Display confidence.* I can already hear you asking me, "And just how am I supposed to do that?" Simple: by doing all of the above. The best way to appear confident is to be confident, and the best way to be confident is to be prepared.

A mentor also needs to possess what I call performance stability. Even under conditions of stress, uncertainty, or just plain chaos, a mentor has to remain calm. Easier said than done? Not necessarily— not if you always keep a few things in mind.

First of all, never forget that all jobs produce their share of stress; it comes with the territory of having a job in the first place. Secondly, all stress disappears with time. Nothing's ever as bad, in retrospect, as it seemed at the time. Most people cave in under pressure because they can't keep things in perspective, and yet there are few truer words in the Bible than the old Hebraic maxim, "This too shall pass." Stress is temporary and should be treated as such. The mentor stabilizes his people by keeping them aware of this fact.

Most business stressors come from competing demands. We panic when we realize we can't cover everything, and as a result, we cover nothing. But this is precisely how not to operate under

stress. Instead, we must prioritize, thereby focusing on the most important demands and letting the least important things go. In this way, something gets

"Those two shots were great Mr. Tell– now, let's discuss the next one."

done rather than nothing. Usually the big things are the primary source of the all stress anyway, while the little things merely nag.

Stress requires patience, organization and—most of all—a sense of humor. Because, in the end, no matter how bad it seems now, it will only seem half that bad tomorrow.

Finally, a mentor must have good inner work standards. A mentor must have exacting personal standards. She should define for herself her own standards, for those who set their own standards tend to set higher ones than those imposed from the outside (Remember Milt Campbell?).

To test a manager's work standards, ask the following questions:

• Does the manager demonstrate a desire to perform at or near the limits of capability most the time, even when a lesser effort would be acceptable?

- Does the manager consistently perform at the height of his or her capabilities?

- Does the manager work to satisfy his or her own criteria, even when this means doing more than is required?

A mentor should always be able to assess fairly his own strengths and weaknesses. For example, if a mentor feels his people aren't always getting the message, he needs to assess his own communication skills. He may learn that, although he's a great listener—he has no problem understanding his people's needs—he may nevertheless be a poor speaker. He might then go out and buy books on effective communication, or he might listen to public speaking tapes in his car on the way to work. Not only will skill increase, but his employees will see the extra effort he has made. An example such as that has a wonderful tendency to become contagious.

ONE CAVEAT BEFORE MOVING ON

A mentorship program begins and ends with the mentors themselves. They *must* be willing to practice what they preach if they ever hope to inspire others. If everyone in the organization strives for improvement, there's no way on earth that everyone won't benefit in some way. Thus improvement becomes the cornerstone of Mentor Management. Ultimately, by committing management to the improvement of its people, an organization begins to make the most important long-term investment it can make.

Now that we've covered the essential ideas behind mentor management, let's now examine mentorship in action . . .

Chapter Eight:

DEVELOPING DAGWOOD

Doce ut disceras
(Teach so that you might learn)

Back in the early Eighties, managers from all over the country suddenly began referring to themselves as "coaches." No longer content with being mere middle men in a vast organization, these managers began seeing themselves as the "field general" of a "winning team" whose primary goal was "producing winners."

For the most part, this new coaching mentality was a change for the better. At least now managers had found a viable way to promote teamwork. On the other hand, many of these same managers took the term "coach" a bit too literally, drawing their inspiration from the Vince Lombardi School of Team Management, where Winning Is Everything. In the end, there was little noticeable difference between the new "coach" and the old dictatorial "manager."

I tell you this as background for the following story. At this time I was observing one of my own managers, a fierce grizzly bear of a guy who was something of a cross between Mr. Dithers and Knute Rockne. He was trying to coach a sales representative who'd performed poorly for the last three quarters. The scene went something like this:

"Dagwood," he said, pointing to a chair, "C'mere and sit down, son. Now, if I remember correctly—and put that sandwich down, for Pete's sake!—anyway, when you came to work for me, you and I talked about how we expect you to make 100% of your objectives. That ring a bell with you? Well, I've got your numbers right here. You're supposed to sell 60 grand worth of telephone systems, but I see here you're only selling 45. That's only 75% of your objectives, Dagwood. Now, did you or did you not commit to making 100% of your quota?"

Dagwood swallowed hard, then nodded his head in agreement.

"That's what I thought. And I think it's probably fair to say that you didn't come here to fail—am I right?"

Again Dagwood agreed.

"Then you've gotta stop achieving only 75% of your quota, boy! You hear me? Are you prepared to renew your 100% commitment?"

Dagwood sat up straight, nodded his head and very resolutely affirmed, "Yes, I am!"

"Well, okay then! That's just what I wanted to hear! Now, take your sandwich with you and get back to work—I know you can do it!"

Dagwood left the room looking very charged and motivated. Meanwhile his boss turned to me and gave a big, satisfied grin, as if to say, "I guess I solved that little problem!"

I refrained from strangling him, but believe me I wanted to. Because what do you think happened after Dagwood left the room?

Simple: he got about half way down the hallway, stopped, scratched his head, and then said to himself, "Now how the heck am I going to make my objectives?" Not only did Dagwood not know how he was going to meet his quota, chances are, he had no idea why he wasn't getting the job done in the first place!

His boss had identified the problem, sure, but not the source of the problem. In other words, Dagwood's boss had failed to locate the skill deficiency preventing him from making 100% of his objectives.

I knew that this was true, by the way, because there were twenty-two other people in the sales office who were doing better. So his performance was not a matter of unrealistic expectations. Rather, his sub-par performance was a combination of poor skills on his part and poor skills-management on the part of his boss.

I helped solve Dagwood's problem by showing his boss how to be less of a rah-rah coach and more of a mentor—which in the end helped both Dagwood and his boss. So fix yourself a triple-decker sandwich and settle in on the couch, because I'd like to spend the rest of this chapter showing you how to teach an old Dagwood new tricks.

T.E.A.C.H.I.N.G. AN OLD DAGWOOD NEW TRICKS

For managers to become mentors, they first must raise their people's proficiency levels. There's a simple process for doing this, which breaks down to an 8-step program:

1) **T**each yourself the relevant job skills.

2) **E**xamine the employee in action.

3) **A**ssess the employee quickly and fairly.

4) **C**o-develop a specific action plan.

5) **H**elp the employee stay on track.

6) **I**nvolve the employee in setting objectives.

7) **N**otify the employee periodically about progress.

8) **G**ive formalized feedback.

I'm sure you noticed that these steps spell out the word T.E.A.C.H.I.N.G. Aside from providing a handy little mnemonic, TEACHING gives us a great method for enhancing job performance—mainly because it favors process over product. Whereas coaches tend to focus too much on goals (product), teachers concentrate on developing the skills (process) that ultimately achieve those goals. In fact,

Before managers can motivate, they first must teach and evaluate.

Because Mentor Management attacks the job at the level of skills, it always stays focused upon the job itself. By improving skills, the mentor can improve both people and performance.

Dagwood's boss probably won't convince Dagwood to stop eating those enormous sandwiches at work; however, by getting Dagwood to work on his skills, this same mentor might just teach Dagwood how to achieve 100% of his objectives. And if that doesn't work, then the mentor can take care of the problem the way teachers always do: via the report card. We'll take care of all of that when we get to the evaluation stage a little later on, but for right now, let's find out what TEACHING really involves.

1) Teach yourself the relevant job skills.

When Dagwood's boss yelled, "Go out there and do better!" he might as well have said nothing at all because a statement like that pretty much says nothing. Or at least nothing useful. Whereas Dagwood needed advice, all he got was a pep talk. He already knew he needed to do better; he just didn't know how. As I found out later, Dagwood's manager didn't know that Dagwood had a skill deficiency because he didn't really know what skills were needed to perform Dagwood's job. All of which explains why he had nothing to add to his little pep talk.

A mentor, on the other hand, focuses directly on job skills, for he understands that improving performance means improving skills. The best way to improve someone else's skills is to acquire proficiency in those skills yourself. In short, there's no getting around the fact that

Mentors can only teach what they already know.

It's quite simple, really: to achieve authority and credibility in the work place, we must know not only the requisite skills for each job, but also the best way to improve them. In short, we must attempt to master the skills ourselves.

This process will work for just about any managing job. If you're a manager at a restaurant, for example, you might not be a very good line cook yourself, but it wouldn't hurt to spend a week or two behind the line to find out what a cook's job entails. It wouldn't hurt either to look around at some of the best cooks to see what they do well and find out how they got to be that way. It wouldn't hurt also to read a few books on the subject, or if that's not your style, to talk to managers who have successfully trained and developed good cooks.

Fortunately, most managers earn their positions by first serving in the trenches. Someone who's been promoted from a salesperson to a manager, for instance, knows exactly what salespeople go through; she knows the skills required for the job and the obstacles that obstruct progress. Because of her experience, she'll probably make a good sales manager, too.

A mentor's best friend is knowledge gained from experience. Never underestimate it. On the other hand, if you find yourself in charge of a group of people who perform tasks outside your own experience, there's only one thing to do: *learn the tasks yourself.*

How can a restaurant manager insist that his fry cook isn't working up to potential if he's never worked the fry station himself? For all this manager knows, his fry cook's Speedy Gonzales—or Mr. Magoo.

A mentor doesn't necessarily have to master the skills of everyone's job, but he does need to appreciate them. Before he can properly judge his employee, then, a mentor must be familiar with the skills required to reach a level of mastery in a given job.

Ultimately, the mentor must acquire enough expertise in the job so that she can teach it well. If that sounds like a huge undertaking, just remember this little paradox, a surprising piece of truth that every teacher will corroborate: the best way to master something is to teach it. Once the mentor learns how the job's done and, more importantly, how the job is done well, only then is he ready to assign a skill level associated with that job. (See Appendix C for a method for assessing the skill level of a manager.)

Let's say, for instance, that Dagwood's boss has read the "Art of Business." As a result, he now knows that a good sales person must possess excellent planning, listening, and speaking skills.

Although it's true that Dagwood needs some writing skills—for proposals, memos, reports and so on—they aren't as necessary for the job as planning, listening, and speaking; thus this mentor assigns writing a lower skill rating. After the mentor has assessed all the qualities needed for the job, and after he has rated these skills in order of importance, then he's ready to go out and observe Dagwood actually performing them.

2) Examine the employee in action.

As everyone knows, managers observe people. What everyone doesn't know is what, precisely, they're supposed to observe. Too many managers focus entirely on the individual, thereby confusing style with substance.

Good mentors, on the other hand, focus on the job itself, concentrating less on the performer and more on the performance. As we learned in step one, in order to analyze performance we must break down the job into its various stages and then acquire familiarity with all the requisite job skills. In step two, then, we must keep those skills in mind as we observe and assess our people in action.

Let's return to Dagwood to see how this process works. After teaching himself the skills necessary for Dagwood's job, Dagwood's boss then goes out on the job with Dagwood. Immediately, the boss begins to notice certain things:

"Okay," he thinks to himself, "Dagwood's got great notes every time he goes out on a call, so I know he's a great planner. He's personable, friendly, knowledgeable about his product, and his talking skills are fine. Up front he's strong, but he's weak at the end. In other words, he has a hard time closing."

Once the boss has figured this out—that is, once he has narrowed the problem down—he can observe the problem area more closely. He does this once, twice, three times, as many times it takes to make an accurate assessment of Dagwood's closing skills.

Suppose after a few of these observations he learns, to his surprise, that the problem's not so much the close, but the middle stages of the sale. Then it hits him: Dagwood's not just a good talker, he's too good a talker. In other words, the boss has located Dagwood's skill deficiency: listening.

"Now I know his problem," the boss reasons. "The guy never listens. He talks when he should be gathering WIIFMs. Sometimes he even cuts off the buyer while she's trying to tell him what she needs!"

Then the boss begins to notice other problems along this line:

"He's always telling other salespeople about his calls, but he never hangs around to listen to theirs; he cuts off secretaries when they try to give him his messages; he never knows what time meetings are; and he often has to ask someone else to repeat what he didn't hear in the boardroom."

Clearly, Dagwood's boss has discovered what's keeping Dagwood from achieving his objectives. But once he has uncovered the problem, he doesn't despair—it's not as if Dagwood's a hyperverbal psychopath; the poor guy just needs to improve his listening skills. Instead, the boss starts thinking about two things: a) how he's going to present the problem to Dagwood, and b) how they both can come up with a plan to fix it. Only when he has worked out the details of these two things is he ready to meet with his employee.

3) Assess the employee quickly and fairly.

The two most important features of an employee assessment are its timeliness and its fairness. First and foremost, a mentor should try to provide timely feedback, preferably right after an observation, while the assessment's still clear in her head. Even if the observation revealed no serious problems, the mentor should never pass up an opportunity to offer praise when it's due.

Of course, timeliness is even more important when there are problems, for the longer the mentor waits to provide feedback, the longer that problem thrives within the organization. And as all good teachers know, the deeper a bad habit takes root, the harder it is to extirpate. In the end, timeliness allows the mentor to illustrate the skill deficiency with concrete, recent examples, while it provides the advisee with a fresh and current assessment of his or her performance.

Secondly, a mentor should try to make her assessment as fair as possible, for the fairer the assessment, the more receptive an individual will be to criticism. I recommend a performance assessment take the following form:

Stress the positive and highlight the negative.

"And now, da award for da most stolen bases goes to... Vinny Six-fingers."

No matter how hard they have to dig, mentors should first tell their advisees what they're doing well. There's a couple of reasons behind this logic. For one thing, when we first give somebody positive feedback, we create a more receptive atmosphere for criticism.

Secondly, prefacing our criticism with praise changes the very nature of that criticism. In a sense, we're asking our employees to bring a deficient skill up to the same level of excellence they've already achieved elsewhere. The employee's criteria for success becomes internal rather than external, i.e. his goals are self-generated rather than arbitrarily imposed from the outside.

To see this technique in action, let's return to Dagwood's boss once more. After teaching himself the skills of the job and examining his employee on the job, the boss must now assess Dagwood in person. His assessment might run something like this:

"C'mon in, Dagwood. Take a seat. Hey, did you hear that noise? I think that's your arteries screaming from that enormous darn sandwich you just swallowed!

"Anyway, I wanted to give you a little feedback on that account we did yesterday. I looked over your notes and I saw that you were very well prepared. Preparation, as you know, is crucial to an effective sale, and you certainly did your homework. You knew this guy inside and out. Also, I must say, you did an excellent job identifying yourself and presenting the company's strengths. The customer knew why you were there and what our company had to offer him. You're a very personable and knowledgeable salesperson, and I want you to continue presenting yourself like that."

The boss waits here as Dagwood beams and soaks up all this praise. Then the boss says, "What I'd like to talk to you about today concerns improving your listening skills . . ."

See the difference? If Dagwood takes any pride in his thorough presentation skills—which, after his boss's glowing testimonial, he should—he can now honor this achievement by raising his listening skills to the same level. Chances are, Dagwood will amble out of that meeting thinking to himself,

"So that's what's wrong. The reason I'm not closing is because I'm not listening. But of course: it's so obvious. After all, it's not like Blondie hasn't told me the same thing a million times . . ."

4) Co-develop a specific action plan.

But we can't let Dagwood out the door just yet. While the above technique's a judicious way to inform Dagwood of his problem, it doesn't do much else. For instance, the Vince Lombardi coach might shout "Dagwood! You don't listen! Listen better!" and be done with it. But that's little better than saying "Go out there and do better." What we need now is an action plan to improve the deficient skill.

An action plan is really nothing more than a step-by-step method for improving a given skill set. The key is to get as specific as possible. Once again, less is more. In other words, don't try to do too much all at once.

If a particular job requires twenty skills, there's no way you can fix all twenty in a single shot. At best you can fix two, maybe three skill sets at a time. Once they're taken care of, however, you can move on to one or more of the remaining eighteen.

When choosing which skills to work on, I like to balance the good with the bad. Experience shows that working on already strong skills increases confidence, which can in turn improve weaker aspects of job performance. Thus, once Dagwood has improved his listening skills, he might turn back to those preparation skills he has already mastered. For instance, how might these skills be enhanced now that his ears are wide-open?

Most importantly, Dagwood must be included in the development of the plan. In fact, getting the other person involved is what separates a teacher from a teller. Like the proverbial horse led to water, your employee is not necessarily going to swallow everything you give him or her. Which is why it's important that you both agree on a) the problem, and b) the proper way to fix it. In this way, the action plan becomes a contract between mentor and advisee in which both have a stake.

Thus, after accentuating the positive and highlighting the negative, Dagwood's boss now says:

"Okay Dagwood, here's what I want you to do: in your next three sales calls—Dagwood, stop eating for a minute and write this down!— ask your clients this question: 'Can you tell me the five year plan for your company?' Then I want you to write down what they tell you. And lastly, I want you to start counting to five after you ask each question. That's all: Make your pitch and count silently to five. Now, how about you? How do you think you might help improve your listening skills?"

Dagwood swallows back a pickle, scratches his head and says,

"Gee whiz, I dunno, boss. I guess I could listen to these audio tapes by Tom Hopkins my wife bought me last Christmas. They're all about, you know, listening and stuff, except that I've never really listened to them yet. So I guess I could do that. At least it would make her happy."

"Great!" the boss replies. "And I'll tell you something else: If you listen to those tapes, I promise to go out with you on a few sales calls. That way I can see what kind of progress you're making. But I'll only go if you listen to those tapes, you understand?"

Dagwood looks up from his sandwich and says, "What? I'm sorry, I missed that last thing you said . . ."

Oh well. At least it's a start. At least Dagwood walks out feeling good about the things he does well; moreover, he now knows what skills he needs to improve and how he's going to improve them.

5) Help the employee stay on track.

Of course, the job of mentoring can't end with one meeting. Mentors must habitually follow-up on any development plan they've set into motion. And I do mean "habitually." Get in the habit of maintaining an on-going dialogue with your employees!

As a mentor, we must stay in contact with our advisees to chart their progress and to answer any questions that might pop up. And this doesn't always have to be a great time-consumer. Sometimes all it takes is a quick comment in the hallway:

"Hey, Dagwood, how are those Hopkins tapes coming along?"

Dagwood either looks down at the ground and kicks some imaginary dirt, or he says, grinning: "What? I wasn't listening." In effect, we're simply encouraging each employee to take on the responsibility for his or her own improvement.

So that's all five steps to the skills development program. Remember, all you have to do is TEACH:

- **T**each yourself the relevant job skills.

- **E**xamine the employee in action.

- **A**ssess the employee quickly and fairly.

- **C**o-develop a specific action plan.

- **H**elp the employee stay on track.

Before moving on to evaluation, however, I would like to add one final word on skills development: Ultimately, there's no end to this process. That's why it's called a "process" in the first place.

Every time you and your employees meet a new challenge, you'll find another challenge waiting right around that corner. But that's exactly as it should be. Once your employees regard self-improvement as a means rather than an end, then your job as a mentor becomes much more definitive—and rewarding. As my father used to say to me on long automobile rides, "Don't be so impatient, Bob. Don't you know that half the fun's getting there?"

EVALUATING DAGWOOD'S VALUE

Everyone in business gets evaluated, and everyone, to some degree or another, hates it. Yet as any manager knows, giving evaluations is often as unpleasant as receiving them. For evaluator and evaluated alike, the evaluation process can be a painful and anxiety-producing experience.

The last three steps, then, the "ING" of TEACHING, are meant to take some of the sting out of this important aspect of a manager's job. While no single innovation can remove all the unpleasant aspects of evaluating (such as having to fire someone), a formal system that is fair, objective, and easily understood can work to the benefit of all. (For those of you who find forms as useful guidelines, Appendix B and C contain an evaluation process based on the material in this chapter).

6) Involve the employee in setting objectives.

What exactly are we trying to accomplish when we evaluate someone? First of all, we want our employees to know how well (or how badly) they're performing their jobs. Second, we want them to know if they can expect rewards, such as job promotions or raises. But most importantly, we evaluate them to make sure management and labor are reading from the same page.

All three goals share a deep-rooted belief in open and honest dialogue between the evaluator and the evaluated. An evaluation, then, ought to produce a mutually agreed-upon set of objectives for both management and staff. The main goal, in other words, is partnership. Mentors and employees must not only agree on the projected goals but also co-develop a plan to achieve those goals.

Mentors must initiate the process by actively seeking input from the person doing the job. By soliciting input, mentors accomplish two things: first, they include their employees in the building process; second, they decrease their own workload, since the employees help set the objectives.

Even better, this method ensures that mentor and employee have a shared interest in the improvement process; since both parties had a stake in creating the objectives, both have invested interests in meeting these same objectives.

How do we involve employees from the start? Believe it or not, by letting our employees help write their own job descriptions. Managers make a great error when they fail to give the employee any input. Consequently, everything that employee does is something the manager has told her to do. If she were a machine this wouldn't be a problem, but she's not; instead, she's a human being with far more versatility than any machine could ever hope to have. A manager who defines a job too strictly fails to take advantage of this versatility.

For example, Dagwood's new job description might demand he make widgets—sixty-five a-day, to be exact. Dagwood has a question about this number, but his boss has made it clear: sixty-five widgets a day. If the discussion ends there, then that's all that boss will ever get: sixty-five widgets a day—no more, no less.

But what if Dagwood knows how to make, say, seventy-two widgets a day? Or what if, at his previous place of employment, he was taught how to make sixty widgets a day and help with inventory at the same time?

Without Dagwoods input, not only will that boss get seven less widgets a day, but Dagwood will have no incentive to go that extra step. With no input, he has no personal goals, and no reason to treat his job as anything other than an arbitrary, impersonal task.

After we and the employee write the job description, we must then co-establish the objectives implied in that description. We never want our people to go home for the weekend and look back on the week and say, "Ah, I accomplished my job description."

Rather, we want them to be thinking about their objectives, about accomplishing their week's goals. We do this by co-developing a short-term and a long-term set of objectives.

Short-term objectives are job specific—you and your people can best define what short-term objectives apply to each job. Long-term objectives, on the other hand, involve foresight and career planning. In fact, consider these objectives as part of an employee's "Career Development."

If a mentor knows where his advisee wants to go within the corporation, then she can build this incentive into the job from the start. If the employee wants to move up the corporate ladder, for instance, the mentor can persuade him to concentrate on those skills that will facilitate this movement.

Thus the promise of career advancement motivates the employee to improve those ear-marked skills. Not only does the employee work harder, but the mentor accomplishes her primary goal: employee development. That's what we call a Win-Win situation.

By the way, "Career Development" doesn't necessarily entail vertical advancement or monetary compensation. Career movement also occurs horizontally within a fixed job set. In fact, this kind of career development can be a mentor's most effective motivational tool. As the employee masters new skills, his potential for later advancement increases; meanwhile, his job remains a challenge even as his personal stake in the company deepens.

Moreover, a manager can help her advisee even in those organizations where the possibilities for career advancement are limited. A manager at a fast-food restaurant, for example, might have a college student who wants to be a lawyer some day. Although this manager can't promote this employee to the state bar, she can work around the employee's college schedule so that the guy can both work and study. Not only will the manager help the student on his way to law school, she'll have an appreciative, motivated employee on her hands the whole time he's there. Yet another Win-Win situation.

Learning to build short-term and long-term objectives into a job description also make it a lot easier when evaluation time comes. If Dagwood wants to be a manager some day, his boss can say things like, "Dagwood, you've done such a great job in improving your listening skills that I think you're well on your way to becoming a fine manager."

Now that's real mentoring.

7) Notify employee with periodic progress reports.

Now it's time to tackle those darn evaluations. My best advice? Don't put them off until the end of the year. Rather, try to stagger the evaluations over the course of the year, i.e., from January to March, from March to June, etc.

This technique has a variety of advantages. For one thing, a single, massive year-end evaluation effort can bring your business to a grinding halt. For another, employees deserve more feedback. When we evaluate once a year, we squander numerous opportunities to inform our people about their progress.

For instance, here's a far too common business scenario: For an entire business cycle, Dagwood has achieved 110% of his objectives; thus he rightly assumes he's doing fine. But then comes his yearly evaluation. Dagwood walks into the boss' office figuring he's got a good bonus coming, but hears this instead:

"Well, my boy, I've got some bad news. Although you've got admirable sales results this year, the fact is we've had lots of customers complaining about you. What's more, a lot of your co-workers say you're not much of a team player. To be frank, you aggravate a lot of people around the office.

"Your peer evaluations are the lowest I've seen in ten years of managing! Look at this: You scored at the bottom in every category—helpfulness, courtesy, support and so on. I can't, with a good conscience, grant you a salary increase—not until you improve your attitude."

Now it's time for Dagwood to go through the roof. If he doesn't quit right then and there, he's going to be one unhappy camper for a good part of the next evaluating cycle.

But Dagwood's not the one to blame here. It's not his fault he didn't know what a pain in the neck he was being. In fact, since he never got a chance to correct his behavior, it's not even his fault he's not getting a raise.

"Your attitude Harv, is at 120%—however, in this organization the requirement for that category is in the 126 to 132% range."

Rather, the blame goes to his boss for not giving him an opportunity to improve his attitude. Apparently the boss chose to wait until year's end to unleash the bad news, all so he could avoid playing the heavy. He also should have been soliciting input from Dagwood's co-workers all year long. Furthermore—out of fairness to Dagwood and respect for the other employees whom Dagwood made miserable—he should've addressed the problem as soon as he heard about it.

Periodic evaluations, on the other hand, can avoid all of the above problems. In the long run, they take less time, reveal problems early and maintain a useful and productive dialogue between managers and employees.

But perhaps the best reason to conduct periodic evaluations is because they guarantee

No surprises at year's end.

Our employees deserve to know where they stand: they need to know their future goals, current progress, areas still requiring improvement and, finally, compensation (if any) for meeting their annual objectives.

Four evaluations per year should be manageable enough for even a busy manager. Here's a suggested format for the evaluation process:

- At the beginning of each quarter, hold a personal meeting with each employee and develop both a developmental action plan and a career plan; ideally, the two would dovetail. In other words, try to improve those skills that would help the employee achieve his or her larger career goals.

- Then at the beginning of each subsequent quarter meet with the employee again and check on his or her progress (a simple one-sentence record of the meeting usually does the trick).

- Finally, at the end of the year, compare the goals outlined in the beginning of the year with the goals achieved at year's end.

As simple a process as this is, its formality plays an important role. By making the evaluation process formal we demonstrate our serious commitment to the improvement of each and every person in the organization. (For a handy schemata of this quarterly evaluation process, see Appendix D.)

8) Give formalized feedback.

As unpleasant as evaluating might sometimes seem, the fact remains: we can't improve somebody if we're not vigilant. We can't expect improvement without offering feedback, and that leads us to the final step of TEACHING.

Although verbal feedback is useful and necessary, a manager must keep track of her people on paper, too. Documentation is a good way to avoid not only legal hassles but the above Dagwood scenario as well, where Dagwood's only real choice is to quit or stay on as a potential troublemaker.

Paperwork doesn't have to resemble an IRS tax form, either. When I use the term "formalized," all I'm suggesting is that we take out a little sheet of blue-lined paper and write down exactly what was said at the meeting and what was agreed upon by both parties.

Formalized feedback's especially useful should things get out of hand. It can make sure that the unpleasant aspects of the job—i.e. firing, giving warnings, or imposing consequences—are always based on rational, objective criteria. Let's say Dagwood's year-end review comes around and he must be told the bad news:

"What!" he screams. "How dare you not give me the raise I deserve?!"

In response, the boss merely pulls out Dagwood's folder and displays the evaluation sheets.

"Well," the boss says, "for starters, do you remember this form from last March? No? But you signed your name right here. See? We said you needed to improve your listening skills.

"We agreed you would listen to the Hopkins tapes, and that I'd go out on some calls with you. Well, I did go out on some calls, but I didn't see any substantial efforts on your part to improve.

"In the next meeting, in June, we agreed that you were still not working on these skills. Granted, in October you did finally start to show improvement, but it took you a little too long to get it in gear. I'm not saying there hasn't been improvement, but it took you too long, and that's why you're not getting a 10% raise."

Now that's a pretty hard case to argue against. It's fair, reasonable and objective. Dagwood has no one to blame but himself.

Of course, evaluating doesn't need to be as negative as that, especially if everybody understands that the final goal of evaluation is improvement. And that's better than a roomful of automatons mindlessly under-performing their humdrum jobs.

But now we've touched on another area, which I will cover in the next—and concluding—chapter: how to design the best possible work environment.

Chapter Nine:

EMPOWERING ENVIRONMENTS

Before moving on to the final component of mentor management, ask yourself these five questions:

1) What does empowerment mean to you?

2) Do your people feel empowered (whatever that means)?

3) Would you characterize your present work environment as positive?

4) Are your people afraid to take risks?

5) Have you ever been to Cincinnati—oh, wait, I think I used that one already—Um . . . ever been to Syracuse?

With the exception of number five, these questions help assess what kind of work environment you're currently fostering. Keep your answers in mind as you go through this chapter and you'll discover what changes must be made to turn your present work situation into an empowering environment. As for that last question . . . well, you guessed it—who cares? Hello? Ever hear of a learning curve?

EMPOWERMENT SHMOWERMENT

As is the case with most buzzwords in American business, the more people use the word "empowerment," the less sense it seems to make. The word's generated so much confusion and misapprehension that many level-headed people have written it off as the latest trend, as a vague and insubstantial idea sounding good in theory but not in practice.

To clear up the confusion, I'd like to share an experience concerning empowerment. Ironically, it concerns a guy named Rollie, the first person I ever had to fire.

Back in 1983, my people were doing very well. Every person on my sales team was achieving above and beyond their objectives—except one. This was Rollie, consistently the low man on the totem pole.

His lack of achievement defied common sense. Rollie was a bright guy with loads of talent, yet he never managed to achieve even the pack average. We tried everything to improve his performance. I assigned two different managers to work on his skills, and when that didn't work, I took him on myself.

I thought, "Surely I, Bob Focazio, can teach this guy the art of selling. In fact, I'm soooooo good that, by virtue of my own supreme example, I alone will be able to empower him."

Well, it didn't work. Despite my best efforts, Rollie continued to lag behind. It was time to face facts: Rollie simply had to go. I called him into my office and said,

"Rollie, I'm sorry I have to tell you this, but we just don't have a match here. I honestly feel bad—you work extremely hard, but you always come in last. We've tried to work on your skills, but you just aren't at the level you should be. So, Rollie, unfortunately we have to let you go."

He shocked me with his answer.

"Bob," he said, "thank you. The fact of the matter is, I hate this job. I hate sales. I hate being a salesman."

I was stunned.

"You see," he continued, "if I'd quit on my own my wife would've killed me. Yet all I've ever wanted to do is go to law school. I want to be a lawyer, not a salesman. And now I've finally got the chance to do what I always wanted to do."

I realized then that I had made a typical managerial mistake. No matter how much we all tried to empower him, Rollie was never going to become a salesperson. Why? Because he possessed neither the desire nor the aptitude to be one.

Three people were trying to make a square peg fit into a round hole. And therein lay the problem. Too many managers think they can "empower" someone simply by pointing a finger in the right direction and saying "Now you do it." But it doesn't work that way. For all his unlimited cosmic strength, Superman can't do a single thing to make Jimmy Olsen fly. Jimmy Olsen can put on a blue suit and a cape and stand at the edge of a cliff from now until doomsday, and nothing will launch him over that chasm.

Clearly, it's time either to clear up the confusion over empowerment or to invent a new word. The problem lies in the fact that too many people think empowerment's a verb. In other words, managers make the same mistake I made with Rollie. I thought empowerment meant "to empower" people, as if a manager were some kind of motivational Superman with transferable super-powers.

Managers have to realize they can't empower by edict. Why? Because job performance is really a combination of aptitude and attitude. We can't really change someone's aptitude for a given task, and altering their attitude's almost as difficult.

Aptitude measures a person's capabilities. Thus Jimmy Olsen will never be able to jump more than seven feet, Superman or no Superman. As for attitude, if a person believes he can't jump more than seven feet, it's probably because he's been told over and over again that he can't. Ten years of psychotherapy might alter that conviction, but not much else.

In fact, serious psychological factors such as attitude and aptitude often can't be altered by anyone, let alone by a boss. Yet this is exactly what managers try to do when they use "empowerment" as a verb: they try to change somebody's attitude or aptitude and then wonder why they fail.

Rather, empowerment is a noun. It's a quality, a perception, but most of all it's an atmosphere where people feel empowered. The key to empowerment, then, lies in understanding the importance of environment. While managers can't force their people to improve—particularly if those people lack the inner desire to do so—they can nevertheless influence that desire, especially if they foster the right work environment.

Sometimes creating the right environment involves nothing more than allowing people to make changes, take chances, work hard and improve. Sometimes the right environment's a place where people can question the limits of their aptitude without fear of penalty for failure. Or sometimes it's a place where people can feel better about what they do, and perhaps even who they are.

A manager can take control of all these things. He may not be able to empower people by virtue of his dynamic personality and iron will, but he can

Create an environment in which people can empower themselves.

A business setting should be a learning environment, a place where everybody's striving to grow personally and professionally. How do we create this ideal learning environment? It's time to return to those three principles you learned back in the first section and put them all back together. The same three rules apply here, only this time they have been modified to apply to your work environment. Follow these simple rules and you'll find that creating an empowering environment is as easy as 1-2-3.

RULE #1: HELP THEM HAVE FUN

Now I'm not suggesting that people start walking around the

office like clowns with grins painted on their faces, but I am saying a little levity in the workplace can do amazing things to raise people's spirits, which ultimately translates into better performances.

There's absolutely no reason that even the busiest environments can't also be fun places to work. The trick here is to understand the difference between work and play:

Work: tolerating abrasive personalities at the office

Play: taking the kids to the beach

Work: attending power lunches

Play: going out to dinner

Work: driving to work in rush hour traffic

Play: four-wheeling up a mountain

Work: sitting in meetings all day

Play: sitting in front of the television all night

Hmm . . . come to think of it, there's not that much that separates the two, is there?

My point is this: What we call play often contains an element of work (and don't tell me a car-full of kids isn't work!). Likewise, work should involve some play.

Work without play will make even the best jobs seem monotonous and boring. Without something to break up the monotony or to release the stress of a job, sooner or later any job will become sheer drudgery. And then we've got a serious case of de-motivation on our hands that no two-week vacation will ever cure. That's why we, as managers, need to create environments that

Balance the serious aspects of the job with some form of play.

As an example, go back to something we discovered way back in Chapter One. Remember that list of de-motivators you came up with back on page 15? Take a few minutes and list the top five things that de-motivate your people. What gets them down? What impedes their progress? What prevents them from having fun at work? (Once again, while you do that I'll hum the tune of final Jeopardy™ in the background.)

MY PEOPLE'S TOP FIVE DE-MOTIVATORS

1. _____

2. _____

3. _____

4. _____

5. _____

Ask your people to compile a similar list. After you've collected their answers, check to see if your answers match theirs. If not, then you've got some adjustments to make. In fact, this discrepancy might be the biggest de-motivator of all! But if you did manage to hit on a few of the key complaints, check to see how many of their answers directly or indirectly point at you.

(If you don't know why this could be a problem, go back to Chapter One and start reading a little more carefully this time. Do not pass Go. Do not collect $200.)

Simply put, as managers we should be the solution, not the problem. If our people feel like we're putting too much pressure on them, we must find ways to ease the tension. We can adjust factors such as these for an immediate improvement in our work environments.

Although other factors—things like customers, red tape, financial burdens or a lousy product—might elude our direct control, they can be controlled indirectly. How? Through play.

By injecting a little laughter into the proceedings, we can rob even the most serious de-motivators of their negative energy. If, for example, your people can't stand the number of forms they have to fill out at the office, make up a joke form and pass it around. Although it might not take care of the problem, it does at least let your people know you're on their side.

There are a number of ways the introduction of a little fun can take the air out of even the most bloated de-motivators. If, for another example, your people find a certain time of year stressful (like, say, tax time at a CPA firm), plan a break for them either in the middle or at the very end of the job. Schedule a company holiday or throw a party. Whatever it takes to let play do its job as a releaser of tension.

It's not as if this idea's new in the history of human affairs. What are holidays but scheduled opportunities to blow off a little steam? Think of Mardi Gras. Think of Halloween. When we allow a little disorder into our otherwise orderly lives, we create a safe haven from all the tensions, pressures and de-motivators that daily sap our energy. Looking for fun ways to solve problems can also help you with your own job stress. Suddenly, a problem becomes a chance to reach for another creative solution instead of another roll of Tums™.

In closing, here are a few additional tips on how to introduce fun into your work environment:

- *Don't be afraid to poke fun at yourself.* It makes you more human. People like working for real people.

- *Set up internal competitive situations where the rewards focus on fun.* For instance, Team A must do Team B's job for a day. Or, the loser of the monthly sales total has to serve breakfast to the winner.

- *Involve families in the rewards business.* Why not give the winning salesperson the day off and enough tickets to take the whole family to the local waterslide? Promise to do the driving while you're at it (just kidding).

- *Encourage your people to be creative.* Let them come up with some of their own ideas for stress relief.

- *Encourage camaraderie among your people.* While a little friendly banter at the water cooler might on the surface look like lost work time, in the end it can considerably improve company morale, not just for the two banterers but for the organization as a whole.

RULE #2: TREAT THEM WITH RESPECT

The key to creating a positive environment's simple if you remember one thing:

All human beings want to be treated with dignity.

Some people know this truth instinctively; others need to have it beaten into them with a wooden spoon. That's how I learned this cardinal lesson: the hard way.

Do you remember when milk used to be delivered from house to house? Well, I do. One day when I was about five or six, my mother, who was in the process of making 50 pounds of spaghetti for my brothers and me, told me to go out and get a gallon of milk from the milkman. I caught up to him, shoved the money in his face and said something like, "Here."

I came back and my mother said. "Bobba, you putta the milk down." I put the milk down on the counter and then she picked up a long wooden spaghetti spoon and gave me a good hard whack on the behind.

"YEE-OWW!" I screamed. "Whatdja do that for, ma?!"

"Because you deserved it! Don'tcha ever taka the milk froma the milkman without saying 'Thank You.' "

"But ma," I insisted, "he's only the milkman!"

To which she nearly broke the spoon over my head. It was then that I learned that it doesn't matter what people do for a living, whether they're the bank president or the cleaning lady, all people should be treated with dignity and respect. (For those of you out there who disagree with me: don't make me take out my spaghetti spoon!)

Although there are many different managerial styles and processes, no process or style can replace a manager's fundamental regard for human dignity. Some bosses may think they can get away with being abusive all the time simply because they're the boss, but if they think they're going to improve productivity, they've got another thing coming.

Monetary compensation might inspire obedience from an employee, but it won't ensure quality performance. Simply put, a manager can't be successful if his people don't feel they're working in a positive environment, for a positive environment provides the best opportunity for increased productivity. Take away that environment, and you get what you pay for: sixty widgets a day and no more.

Remember back in Chapter Two how we tackled de-motivation on the job? If not, take a look at it again. In that section we learned we can empower ourselves by remembering how good we are. The same philosophy applies to our employees.

To create a positive environment, we must help them remember how good they are. By constantly building them up, by turning negatives into positives, we help our people focus on success instead of failure.

The key to creating a positive environment, then, is to remember that people want to think of themselves as successes; they want to feel good about what they do. To help you along, I've listed a few suggestions for creating just such a climate:

1) Affirm how much you need them—If I had to attribute one thing to my success as a manager I'd have to say it was this: people work hard for me. They work hard not because they are afraid to do otherwise, but because they don't want to disappoint me. They know I need them as much they need me. The main reason they strive never to let me down is because I strive to extend them the same courtesy. It's really just a simple application of the Golden Rule: Do unto others as you would have them do unto you. It's not just a nice sentiment, either; experience proves it works.

2) Always stress the positive in evaluating job performance—If you only talk to your people when something's gone wrong, you're fostering a negative environment. Moreover, this kind of behavior violates rule #1. When a manager focuses on the negative all the time, fun becomes almost an impossibility.

3) Don't let office politics taint your working relationships—How many times have you heard people say, "Ah, it's all politics. Frank got promoted because he sucks up to the boss." As everyone knows, performance, not politics, should drive reward systems. And yet still this charge persists.

If you hear such things around your own office, ask yourself this question: How am I assigning rewards? A vague and general compensation plan relies too heavily on the subjective viewpoint of the manager, while an effective compensation plan employs clear-cut qualitative and quantitative criteria.

If you've followed the last couple of chapters closely, you should know by now that your employees need to be periodically

evaluated throughout the year. This is perhaps the best way to eliminate the charge of favoritism among your employees. Otherwise,
everything really is all politics. (And correct me if I'm wrong, but the
last time I checked, Washington D.C. wasn't exactly a model for positive work conditions!)

4) Always look to the future—Remember, people are not only
your greatest asset, they're also your greatest investment. You want
to think of your people in terms of their career, and to remind them
that you're trying to help them reach not just their corporate objectives, but their own personal career objectives as well. (For more
information on how to do this, see Chapter Eight, specifically Step #
7 of the TEACHING Method.)

Strangely enough, if you keep your employees always focused
on their career development, you make yourself obsolete in the
process. But that's exactly as it should be. As with any good teacher,
you want your people eventually to be self-motivated.

Some day you may even be able to sit back and say, "I don't
have any problems today, because: a) my people feel empowered to
answer their own questions; b) they have the skills, the honed skills,
to take care of their jobs; and c) they have the working knowledge to
say, 'I can fix this.' "

5) Be a hands-on mentor—Of course, before your people can
arrive at the point where they don't need you around, they, um . . .
well, they need you around. Unfortunately, too many managers let
their employees train one another. In small doses, this approach can
be effective, but left unchecked it can lead to disaster. Employees are
tempted to tell one another things like, "Forget all that crap you
learned in training. Let me show you a short-cut."

But as I said in the last section, there *are* no short-cuts, because
short-cuts lead to short-changed expectations. A mentor's job, first
and foremost, is to make sure her people learn from the beginning the
proper way to perform the job. The mentor's second job is to follow-
up should they require some help. A mentor, by definition, should
always be there for her people—more than anything else this single
quality will ensure a positive working environment.

RULE #3: SHOW THEM A LITTLE MERCY

As you can see by now, "empowerment" isn't just a buzzword. It's just plain common sense. Contrary to what politicians and Hollywood may think, people are not stupid. Everybody has an aptitude for something. If a mentor can tap into that aptitude and encourage it, then there's no limit to what that employee can accomplish. And that's what showing a little mercy's really all about: giving people the room to live up to their potential.

It didn't exactly require a smack on the behind for me to learn this truth, but it did take a rather outspoken employee of mine to drive the point home.

Back in 1983 I was promoted to general manager and thus received my first experience with unions. On my first day at work, a union steward came up to me in a sweatshirt and jeans and said,

"You're not going to tell us how to run this business. We're going to tell you how to run it."

I thought to myself, "Great. First day, first major headache."

But I didn't let it get me down. Although I was the new guy on the job, I knew better than to think that I knew more than everybody else simply because I wore a suit and tie.

So I said, "I don't necessarily agree that you're going to run everything, but I will tell you this: I do need your input."

Despite a shaky start, our team ended up being amazingly productive. In fact, our union numbers were significantly higher than any other in the organization.

I attribute our success to one simple fact: employee involvement in the decision-making process. At first I didn't understand the importance of this gesture, which explains that shaky start. The person who turned me around was the same union steward.

I asked for input, and boy did she give me input. I'll never forget the day she came into my office and told me I wasn't utilizing our people to their fullest potential.

"Now Bob, " she said, "I know you have a college degree and a Masters degree, while I don't have any of that. The fact of the matter is, I barely made it through high school.

"But do you know something? After five o'clock there isn't a single decision you make out there in the real world that I don't make myself.

"I have to decide where to send my kids to college. I have to decide what car to buy every three years. I have to decide what to buy at the grocery store. I have to prioritize my expenses, separating necessities from luxuries. Everything you decide after 5 o'clock, I decide.

"So tell me, Bob, why is it that every morning at 9 o'clock I'm suddenly treated like I can't make a decision for myself? I make all the decisions you make from 5 p.m. to 9 a.m. every day, but when I'm at work I have to be told how to do the simplest things. Now, can you tell me why that is?"

It was a great question, and I didn't know the answer. But it sure changed the way I managed my people. From then on I decided I was going to let my people help make the decisions that directly concerned them.

I didn't just point my finger and say, "Now you do it." Rather, I simply let those who actually did the job tell me what they thought would improve it. I asked them to speak their minds about what they thought impeded their performance, and then I asked them to come up with creative solutions.

Afterwards, I implemented some of their solutions and, in the process, removed a number of obstacles keeping them from getting their jobs done.

Some impediments were easily removed: they hated being checked up on all the time, for instance, so I made people accountable primarily by their results; and some people hated the repetitiveness of their jobs, so I moved them around to different work stations to break up the monotony.

Other problems proved more difficult. Not surprisingly, the hardest obstacle to overcome was the same one I once had to overcome in myself. That's right: they were afraid to take risks.

What held true in Chapter Three holds true now: the main deterrent to taking risks is fear of failure. Two factors kept my people from taking chances and being creative with their jobs. The first lay within the people themselves. Some of them just didn't want to think for themselves; they feared independence, seeing it as just one more pressure they didn't need. So for these people I eliminated the pressure.

Others did want to be creative but were afraid of sticking by their own ideas. They would step out of the box for a while, but then quickly return to the old safe way. When we looked into the reasons for this behavior, we found the second cause: management.

Several of our managers were quick to impose consequences when somebody tried something and failed. Even if they weren't firing people for failure, they were still putting on the pressure. Sometimes all it took was a sideways glance at an error; other times managers made wisecracks like, "If you mess this up, you might want to start looking for a new job, buster."

But these little things accumulated to create a climate in which people were afraid to fail. In fact, one of the most important things we can do as managers is to

Remove the threat of failure.

If you have a work environment now in which there is no failure, chances are you also have an environment in which there is no fun, no risk-taking, and worst of all, no improvement.

As any teacher, researcher, advertiser or athlete can tell you, new ideas always involve some measure of failure—that's where we get the phrase "trial and error."

My Latin teacher, Sister Mary Dominiani, used to tell us not to be afraid to make errors. Then she'd show us that the Latin root for error is *errare*, which means "to stray." If you don't stray from the right path every now and then, she told us, you won't know what's right about the right path and what's wrong about the wrong one.

It's okay when our people err, because it means they're straying, and when they're straying, they're taking risks. And when they're taking risks, they're trying to improve the way they do their job. In the final analysis, what else could we possibly want or expect from an employee?

HELLO, SYRACUSE

Okay, I guess we've time for one memory of Syracuse, after all. One day while picking up my bags at the Hancock Airport, I got a tap on my shoulder. And lo and behold, it was Rollie, the first guy I ever fired.

To say he caught me off-guard is an understatement. Even though a few years had passed since his firing, the words "disgruntled postal worker" still went off in my head like a siren.

But to my relief, Rollie was beaming. We shook hands and we got to talking. As it turns out, he had graduated from Columbia Law School with honors, and was now a high-powered corporate lawyer.

We talked and laughed about the old days, and when it was time to go, Rollie put his hand on my shoulder and said, "You know, Bob, I'm thinking about suing you."

This time I heard an ambulance siren go off. "But why, Rollie?" I asked. "You're doing great now."

"Why? I'll tell you why: because you delayed my career."

"Huh?" I said, not getting the joke.

"Yeah, you delayed my career. I told you I couldn't quit 'cause my wife would kill me, but the truth is, Bob, I couldn't quit because I knew I would let you down.

"You tried so hard to make me into a salesman that I felt beholden to you somehow. I stayed in that job because of you, and that's why I'm thinking about taking you to court.

"But you know why I can't go through with it? Because although I never did become a salesman, I learned a lot working under you. I learned how to keep trying, how to stay positive and how to laugh when things get too serious.

"Most of all, I learned that you can be a successful professional and a pretty decent human being all at the same time. So for all of that I think I might be able to see it in my heart to forgive you."

He smiled, winked and looked away.

We stood around for a while, hanging our heads and kicking some imaginary dirt, and though we both felt like lingering awhile longer, we knew it was time to go.

AFTERWORD:

I cannot rest from travel; I will drink
Life to the lees.
—From "Ulysses," by Alfred, Lord Tennyson

Just as Odysseus' journey finally reaches a happy conclusion, so too must our managerial odyssey come to an end.

Odysseus winds up his tale settled in Ithake, wiser from all he's experienced and eager to renew his duties. But if you're wondering what ever happened to Odysseus afterward, you're in good company.

Although Homer never took up Odysseus' story again, other writers have (such as yours truly). Unable to resist the temptation to speculate about the life Odysseus led after his triumphant return, these writers wondered to themselves, "How could so restless a spirit as Odysseus settle into a routine and ignore the urgent tug of new challenges?"

In other words, could Homer's immortal story really end "happily ever after"?

Well, not exactly. This is Odysseus we're talking about, after all. The great Italian poet Dante, for instance, asserted that Odysseus

150

never even made it back to Ithake!

Instead, he persuaded his men to voyage westward beyond the Straight of Gilbralter. "Consider well the seed that gave you birth," he told his followers. "You were not made to live your lives as brutes, but to be followers of worth and knowledge."

According to Dante, this speech convinced Odysseus' men to take up his challenge. "I could hardly have held them back," Odysseus tells Dante—a true mentor to the end.

Perhaps the most famous sequel to the Odyssey, however, belongs to the poet Alfred Lord Tennyson. In his famous poem "Ulysses" (*Ulysses* being the Latin name for *Odysseus*), Tennyson imagines an older, wiser Odysseus at home in Ithake, staring out at sea and longing for new challenges.

Although the great wanderer senses his days are coming to an end, his need for action, for fresh experiences and new accomplishments, burns brighter than ever. As he puts it, "How dull it is to pause, to make an end, to rust unburnished, not to shine in use!"

Even though he and his men are quite along in years, Odysseus nevertheless proclaims, "Come, my friends, 'Tis not too late to seek a newer world."

Every conclusion, in other words, discovers new challenges.

And that's also the final message I leave with you. This managerial odyssey has reached an end only in the sense that the book's complete; the challenges it hopes to inspire within you, however, have hopefully just begun.

Like Odysseus, you too must see each ending as another beginning, each met objective as an opportunity for new challenges. Improvement is perpetual, and each day we are inspired anew. The meaning and worth of what we do is found in the doing itself, a truth that we must both affirm to ourselves and demonstrate to those we manage.

Tennyson once said that his poem "Ulysses" expressed his own "need of going forward and braving the struggle of life"; for me, this little book expresses the same belief. But since we began with Odysseus—and since an Odyssey must, by definition, end where it began—it's fitting that Odysseus get the last word.

Harken, then, to the aging Odysseus in his final, triumphant moment:

> ... *though*
> *We are not now that strength which in old days*
> *Moved earth and heaven, that which we are, we are—*
> *One equal temper of heroic hearts,*
> *Made weak by time and fate, but strong in will*
> *To strive, to seek, to find, and not to yield.*

APPENDIX

Appendix A:
12 Ways to Establish Rapport

1) Be Friendly

2) Be Politic: Say things like, "I know you're very busy . . ."

3) Get their name ("and your name is . . .?)

4) Address them by name ("Mr. Bauerlein, I noticed...)

5) Establish credibility

6) Be enthusiastic

7) Listen, Listen, Listen

8) Be sympathetic

9) Be patient

10) Use everyday language

11) Find a common ground

12) Avoid phoniness

Appendix B:
PERFORMANCE PLANNING & EVALUATION

One way to ensure employee satisfaction is by planning performance objectives and monitoring performance throughout the plan year. Accomplish this through Performance Planning & Evaluation [PP&E]. PP&E has four primary goals:

- To develop practical performance objectives

- To help employees achieve both individual and group-directed goals

- To evaluate employees and groups throughout the plan year so as to develop and strengthen overall company performance.

- To allocate compensation according to results measured against objectives.

PP&E is divided into three steps: 1) Performance Planning, 2) Performance Reviews, and 3) Performance Evaluation. Below are instructions for completing each step.

1. Performance Planning

At the beginning of each plan year the individual and his or her manager will conduct a joint objective-setting session. At this meeting both parties will document a mutually agreed-upon plan specifying the individual's performance objectives for each part of the yearly performance cycle. All objectives should be listed in order of priority.

It is important that both parties establish realistic and attainable goals that both challenge the individual and take into account his or her specific skills and career objectives. Each goal should be stated in terms of *what* is to be accomplished, rather than *how*. Nevertheless, this document might include performance criteria such as quantity and quality of work to be produced, estimated time frames for completion and acceptable expense levels.

2. Performance Review

As a corollary to the initial performance planning session, managers will also conduct and document quarterly performance reviews. In this way managers can gauge individual performance against stated objectives. These reviews can also eliminate end-of-the-year discrepancies between the employee's expectations and those of management.

To conduct a quarterly review, simply refer back to the original Performance Planning document and, for each responsibility and result, rate the employee's progress for the previous quarter. Each goal should be judged according to the following criteria:

- Far Exceeded Results

- Consistently Exceeded Results

- Occasionally Exceeded Results

- Achieved Results

- Failed to Achieve Results

Furthermore, managers are urged to make an additional record of the individual's progress. This allows managers to rate improvements in greater detail. More importantly, this record can be used by both parties to establish a common understanding of where the individual's performance stands in relation to annual objectives, and what assistance the individual might need in order to shorten the gap between performance and objectives. Modifications in such matters as results, time frames and priorities can also be made at this time.

If the quarterly review obligation is not being met, individuals are encouraged to initiate the process. Nevertheless, managers are ultimately responsible for providing feedback.

NOTE: The review stage of PP&E serves as the first step of Career Management.

3. Performance Evaluation

At the end of each plan year the individual and his or her manager will conduct an end-of-the-year evaluation. In this session, both parties will review the documented quarterly reviews and rate the total results against the stated objectives, first for each area of primary responsibility and then for overall performance. Several factors should be considered in this session, including: 1) difficulty of assignment; 2) necessity of supervisory direction; and 3) the ways in which the results were achieved. This last factor is important as it provides the manager a way to ensure that the individual's performance has not yielded *negative* results.

The manager should then fill-out and sign the year-end Performance Planning & Evaluation form. This document includes the employee's Overall Performance Rating.

After the immediate manager has completed and signed the year-end evaluation—and, if necessary, noted any additional comments—he or she should pass the document on to the next level of management, where it should be reviewed and signed again.

After all of this has been accomplished, the individual and the immediate manager should meet one last time for final feedback. At this session both parties can discuss the overall performance rating, the rationale for assigning the rating, and the strong and weak areas of the individual's annual performance. To indicate that this final meeting has taken place, the individual should add a final signature to the PP&E document.

The *original* document should be filed away in the individual's personnel folder for the next two years. Meanwhile, the individual should be given a *copy* of the signed PP&E document.

Appendix C
CAREER MANAGEMENT

The Career Management program (CM) seeks to accomplish two things at once: first, to develop our employees so that they perform at maximum levels in their current job; and second, to facilitate rapid and meaningful employee movement both laterally and vertically through the company organization.

We determine all career movement by assessing the individual's performance, skill development and overall contribution. We never make career movement decisions solely on the basis of tenure. Both managers and individuals are responsible for maintaining an amiable working environment conducive to rapid career movement and employee development. Nevertheless, each individual is ultimately responsible for his or her own career management. By taking responsibility for his or her own career, the individual can better match interests and skills with available opportunities.

After the individual and his or her manager have conducted the performance planning session, both parties should conduct a Career Development discussion. This session has four major objectives:

- To discuss, openly and honestly, the individual's job performance.

- To formulate a specific and practical action plan for developing the individual's performance and management skills, as appropriate. Care should also be taken to develop ways to improve skills that are already strong.

- To provide a forum in which the individual can freely express his or her desired career direction and test the validity of these desires with the manager.

- To establish an agreement between both parties concerning the steps necessary to move the individual in the desired direction and the time frame best suited to accomplish this goal.

Like PP&E, Career Management is divided into three components: 1) the Employee Skills Evaluation, 2) the Development Action Plan, and 3) the Career Plan. Explanations of all three components can be found on the pages that follow.

1. Employee Skills Evaluation

The Employee Skills Evaluation is the tool by which the individual and his or her manager can formulate practical and tailor-made career and developmental action plans. The evaluation has two parts: the Managerial Skills Evaluation and the Performance Related Evaluation. Both parties use this evaluation to examine the individual's managerial and performance skills as they pertain not only to the current job but also to any future job assignments that might lie on the horizon. (Use the skills in part 4 as a starting place.)

Actually, two sets of evaluations should be filled out. Prior to the career development discussion, both the individual and the manager should complete an Employee Skills Evaluation (both Managerial and Performance Related), with each evaluation done independently of the other. Two different ratings should be applied to each skill:

1. IMPORTANCE TO CURRENT JOB
   5 = Most Important
   1 = Least Important

2. INDIVIDUAL'S PROFICIENCY LEVEL
   5 = Most Proficient
   1 = Least Proficient

To justify the various ratings, both individual and manager should cite illustrative examples from the individual's behavior and performance. In this way the individual and manager can better establish common ground during the discussion process. Total agreement on the ratings, however, is not the final goal. Instead, we hope that the discrepancies between the two evaluations will generate a meaningful discussion about the individual's career expectations and the way in which the manager perceives his or her job performance. Ultimately, the individual and manager should arrive at a consensus about which skills need to be included in the development plan (see below).

2. Developmental Action Plan

The Developmental Action Plan (DAP) serves as the blueprint for performance improvement. All the skills listed on the Employee Skills Evaluation should now be documented on the DAP, with top priority given to those skills rated lower in proficiency than in importance to current job.

Next, the DAP should outline all the steps necessary to improve these targeted skills. Some examples include:

- Self-Study

- New Responsibilities

- Special Assignments

- Coaching

- Training

In conjunction with these steps, the DAP should also list plans for improving those weak performance areas identified during the performance feedback sessions. If any of these latter skills have not already been incorporated into the skills evaluation, they should be incorporated now.

Finally, the DAP should include a clear description of the individual's responsibility for executing these action steps, including a reasonable time frame for completion.

In the end, the DAP is designed to address simultaneously the individual's short and long term career objectives. Depending on the individual's level of development in his or her current job, the DAP can help foster the overall Career Plan, since it can initiate the development of those skills necessary for desired future assignments.

3. Career Plans

Unlike the Employee Skills Evaluation and the Developmental Action Plan, the Career Plan should be filled out by the individual. Afterwards the manager will examine the Career Plan for final approval. All jobs listed in the Career Plan should be listed in the organizational manual; furthermore, the Career Plan should outline the specific functional areas of responsibility demanded by each listed job. This latter information can help the individual and manager evaluate the feasibility of the Career Plan in view of the individual's current job assignment and skill level.

All career discussions should be documented and dated.

Final comments on the Career Plan should indicate the manager's perspective on the individual's capacity for fulfilling the plan. Does the individual need continued development in the current job, or should the proposed movement be supported immediately? The manager's decision should be listed on the Career Plan under one of three possible headings:

- Maintain present assignment

- Move individual laterally within the same level

- Move individual vertically to the next level

Because all career movement is the result of the individual's development and contribution, this entry may—and should—change. When the individual's performance begins to reflect development, he or she may reopen the career planning process with the manager.

In conclusion, a manager's main responsibility is to utilize human resources effectively. Not only will the Employee Development system foster maximum employee performance but it will also facilitate useful and necessary manager/employee communication. In order to get the best results from the system, managers must realize that they are ultimately responsible for:

- Developing *all* subordinates

- Resolving personnel problems

- Ensuring timely project completion

- Devising a career/development plan for each individual

In the end, we feel that the key to managerial success is managing one individual at a time. Each subordinate needs to be given not only a stake in the company's overall success, but a clearly stated—and individualized—set of objectives. The Employee Development system is designed to guarantee both conditions.

4. Definition of Professional Managerial Skills

Communication Skills

- Oral Communications

— Gives effective presentations
— Responds effectively to challenges and questions raised by others
— Projects confidence

- Written Communications

— Organizes ideas logically
— Writes clearly and concisely
— Uses appropriate grammar and style

Interpersonal Skills

- Leadership

— Effectively leads a group to accomplish a task without incurring hostility
— Shows active involvement as part of the team

- Impact

— Is perceived as a role model within peer group
— Makes a positive impression on others

- Flexibility

— Modifies approach to reach a goal
— Modifies style to setting
— Tries alternatives to reach established goal

- Sensitivity

— Perceives cues in the behavior of others toward him or her
— Changes manner appropriately

Personal Skills

- Inner Work Standards

— Maintains high level of work activity
— Always strives to satisfy highest criteria of performance

- Self-Objectivity

— Recognizes strengths
— Recognizes weaknesses

- Performance Stability

— Maintains constant level of performance under conditions of stress, ambiguity or disruption

- Self-Development

— Takes initiative to maximize individual growth

- Results Orientation

— Focuses on goal, not process

Problem-Solving Skills

- Fact Finding

— Effectively elicits required information orally or from written materials to solve a problem or complete a task

- Organizing and Planning

— Sets priorities
— Anticipates and avoids conflicts
— Delegates authority as appropriate
— Follows up to ensure task completion

- Decision-Making

— Makes sound decisions as required, using available information and weighing alternatives
— Willing to take risks for creative problem resolution

Note: These skills are generic to most jobs. Add or delete skills based on your understanding of the job.

Appendix D:
ANNUAL DEVELOPMENT CYCLE

By integrating Performance Planning and Evaluation [PP&E] with Career Management [CM], we can provide a complete system for managing employee development. Managers can thus maintain consistent, open, two-way communication at all times. Below is a diagram illustrating the sequence and relationship of activities associated with each of the program components.

Annual Cycle of Activities

	PP&E	CM
First Quarter	Performance Planning	
Second Quarter	1st Quarter Performance Review	Skills Evaluation; Establish Development Plan; Discuss Career Plan
Third Quarter	2nd Quarter Performance Review	Development/ Career Plan; Update
Fourth Quarter	3rd Quarter Performance Review	Development/ Career Plan
End of Year	Performance Evaluation	Review